Praise for *The Silent Witness of Nazareth*

"*De Joseph numquam satis.* One can never say enough of St. Joseph, nor can one praise him enough. After the Blessed Virgin Mary, he is the highest saint, with prerogatives of grace proportioned to his unique mission. Fr. Lanzetta highlights this mission by studying the whole Josephine mystery with new insights. Joseph "took unto him his wife" (Matt 1:24, DRA) and so anticipated what the beloved disciple would do at the foot of the Cross. I pray that this new publication may be known by many so as to enhance both Josephine theology and Christian devotion to the chaste spouse of the Immaculate Virgin Mary, the holy guardian of the Redeemer, and the patron of the universal Church."

—Bishop Athanasius Schneider,
Archdiocese of Saint Mary in Astana

"Fr. Lanzetta—whose baptismal name is Joseph—provides an extraordinary overview of Catholic doctrine and devotion to St. Joseph in this excellent book. Drawing upon the insights of Scripture, tradition, and the writings of the great Josephologist Fr. Tarcisio Stramare, O.S.J., Lanzetta explores the mystery of the virginal spouse of the Virgin Mary and paternal guardian of Christ. He sheds new light on Joseph's relation to the order of the hypostatic union, his purification from Original Sin, and his participation in the priesthood and redemptive work of Christ. This book will help the faithful know and love St. Joseph more deeply and appreciate his role as 'the prototype of Marian consecration.'"

Robert Fastiggi, Ph.D., Professor of Dogmatic Theology,
Sacred Heart Major Seminary, Detroit, Michigan

"Scholarly and pious, *The Silent Witness of Nazareth* is an exceptional work honoring the great St. Joseph. In our day, the Holy Spirit is increasing the faithful's interest in, and devotion to, the virginal father of Jesus and the chaste husband of Mary. Fr. Lanzetta's book keeps this momentum going, offering fresh and thought-provoking insights into the mystery and magnitude of St. Joseph. Very highly recommended!"

—**Fr. Donald Calloway, M.I.C.,**
Author, *Consecration to St. Joseph*

"Devotion to the Holy Family is inseparable from devotion to Jesus Christ. Yet the Church is suffering through a period of neglect of the Blessed Virgin Mary and of St. Joseph. Perhaps Pope Leo XIV will follow his illustrious predecessor Pope Leo XIII in issuing a Josephine encyclical. Fr. Lanzetta has prepared the way with this rich presentation of traditional Josephology."

—**Matthew Levering,**
James N. Jr. and Mary D. Perry Chair
of Theology, Mundelein Seminary

The Silent Witness of Nazareth

FR. SERAFINO M. LANZETTA

THE SILENT
WITNESS
OF NAZARETH

*St. Joseph: Spouse of Mary,
Powerful Intercessor,
Guardian of the Church*

SOPHIA INSTITUTE PRESS
Manchester, New Hampshire

Sophia Institute Press
Box 5284, Manchester, NH 03108
1-800-888-9344
www.SophiaInstitute.com

Sophia Institute Press® is a registered trademark of Sophia Institute.

paperback ISBN 979-8-88911-554-0
ebook ISBN 979-8-88911-555-7

Library of Congress Control Number: forthcoming

First printing

To the august and chaste St. Joseph,
whose equal on earth and in Heaven,
after the Blessed Virgin Mary,
is not to be found.

In fond memory of
Grandfather Giuseppe

Images in This Book

Unless otherwise specified, images are from
Wikimedia Commons and are in the public domain.

Contents

Foreword

The importance of promoting the knowledge and veneration of St. Joseph stems primarily from his role as patron of the universal Church, which is in need of special help "from on high," especially in these times, in order to overcome the crisis of faith currently afflicting its historical and human elements. Yet, we must also insist on the exemplarity of St. Joseph in relation to fatherhood, both natural and supernatural, or spiritual, since he was chosen from all eternity as the virginal father of the incarnate Word: it is urgent, in fact, to propose St. Joseph ever more "clearly and unmistakably" as a strong model in the face of the endemic "crisis of fatherhood" manifested in the paradigms of the dominant culture.

Moreover, within the small flock of pious souls striving to live devoutly in this neo-pagan Western world, there has been a noteworthy increase in theological interest in St. Joseph, along with a growth of Josephine piety, through the impulse of the Holy Spirit who incessantly leads us "into all the truth" (John 16:13). For these souls, St. Joseph is above all the virginal spouse of Mary, the guide and teacher of Marian spirituality. As Mary leads us to Jesus, so St. Joseph leads us to Mary. However, unlike the cult rendered to Mary, which is based on the solid foundations of four dogmas—the understanding of which is certainly destined to grow—the veneration of St. Joseph has not, until now, enjoyed such solid dogmatic support. The Church has not yet made any pronouncement concerning St. Joseph in such a definitive and irreformable manner. The primary sources of the Josephine veneration, rightly defined as *protodulia*, are therefore Scripture and Tradition, followed by the ordinary Magisterium of the Church and the teaching of the saints, but there are no dogmatic pronouncements which, by their very nature, would express in a certain and irrevocable way the contents of the primary sources.

The "history of dogmas" reflects the "hierarchy of truths." From a logical, essential point of view, there is first the mystery of the triune God, followed by the mystery of the Incarnation, then the mystery of the Mother of the incarnate Word, and finally that of His virginal father, St. Joseph. Clearly, we refer here to a logical, essential order which does not necessarily coincide with the chronological order of the people involved, but which does coincide, as we have just stated, with the history of dogma. In the early centuries, the Church defined the trinitarian and Christological dogmas. Then, at the heart of the great Christological and dogmatic reflections which developed during the age of the Church Fathers, in the fifth century, there appears the figure of Mary, insofar as she is indissolubly united to the mystery of the incarnate Word. At the Council of Ephesus in 431, the divine maternity was defined as a corollary of the Christological dogma of the one Divine Person in Christ.

Similarly, in our own time, at the heart of the age of the Immaculate, inaugurated by the dogma of Pius IX in 1854, the figure of St. Joseph stands out, illuminated, as it were, by a light reflected by the mystery of Mary, in turn illuminated by the mystery of Christ, likewise illumined by the trinitarian mystery. These interlinked mysteries form a "sweet chain that binds us to God."

From the Josephine cult of our holy synaxes, let us move on for a moment to the frenetic industrial warehouses and, in general, to all areas of human work where God's original command (see Gen. 1:28) is fulfilled by man "in the sweat of [his] face" (Gen. 3:19) and also, metaphorically, by the "sweat of his brain." St. Joseph has a rightful place here too, as the patron saint of all workers. The Gospel tells us that he was a craftsman, without indicating his specialization or how he exercised his noble profession. Noble it was, indeed, as Jesus Himself practiced it with His father Joseph, during a certain period of His "hidden life": a sign that, in the work of a craftsman, those human virtues are naturally brought together which are an excellent natural basis for the evangelical virtues: prudent intelligence, persevering strength, fair respect for natural laws and for the rules of one's craft, inventiveness, a balanced relationship with things, and an honest relationship with people.

We can imagine that Joseph too, like Bezalel and Oholiab, was filled "with the spirit of God, with ability and intelligence, with knowledge and all craftsmanship, to devise artistic designs, to work in gold, silver, and bronze, in cutting stones for setting, and in carving wood, for work in every craft" (Exod. 31:3–5). If these two Old Testament artisans were so overflowing with the infused science of building the tent and Ark where God dwelt spiritually, then Joseph must have been all the more overflowing with heavenly gifts, having been chosen from among all men to build, in Nazareth, Bethlehem, and Egypt, the first churches in history, which preserved "the whole fulness of deity ... bodily" (Col. 2:9). Admittedly, we know from mystical, spiritual tradition that, unlike the Ark and the tent, it was neither gold nor precious fabrics that adorned the Holy Family's humble home, since Jesus had chosen the state of the "annihilation" of His divinity, in order to atone for the excesses and the vanity of luxury; but all the same, what harmonious beauty shone forth in this sacred, proto-Christian architecture, inspired by the voluntary poverty of Christ and His most holy mother! Thanks to the choice of this humble style, the requirements of the Holy Family were kept to a minimum, leaving St. Joseph the time and means to devote himself to his daily charitable work in favor of the less fortunate. St. Joseph's charity toward the poor was "unbounded,"[1] and it was in this that all his strength was consumed, as he immolated himself for the love of God and neighbor, thus drinking in advance the chalice of his son's Passion, which he glimpsed thanks to his faith in the prefigurations of the ancient rites.

The evangelical silence surrounding the details of St. Joseph's workaday activities does not prevent us from applying to him, in general, the attribute that the Gospel applies to his person: if Joseph was a "just" man (Matt. 1:19), his way of working must also have been just, the word *just* being equivalent to "holy." Indeed, we cannot but affirm that St. Joseph's work was holy and sanctifying, so much so that, after his prayer, it was his principal means of progressing in the theological virtues and in all the other virtues, which are the irradiation of the splendor of charity. St. Joseph reached the pinnacle of holiness *thanks to*, and not *in spite of*, his work as a craftsman.

To Salome, who had importunately requested that her sons sit on either side of Him in His kingdom, Jesus replied: "To sit at my right hand and at my left is not mine to grant, but it is for those for whom it has been prepared by my Father" (Matt. 20:23). Who are these two illustrious figures who occupy the first two

---

[1] If the charity of Bl. Ludovico da Casoria has been described as "unbounded," how much more so that of St. Joseph must have been (see S. Garofalo, *La carità "sfrenata" del beato Ludovico da Casoria*, Gorle, Italy: Editrice Velar, 2000).

places in the heavenly hierarchy? Jesus intentionally withheld their names, as it was for the living Tradition of the Church to one day unveil their identity: at the right of Christ the King sits the Queen Mother, Mary, which is a dogmatic truth now established, even if not yet *definitorio modo*. And who sits to the left of Christ? A chorus of voices asserts, in ever-increasing unison, that it is none other than the Royal Father, St. Joseph, of the family of David, and this, not because of kinship ties, but because of Joseph's perfect adherence to God's will: "Who is my mother, and who are my brethren?... Whoever does the will of my Father in heaven is my brother, and sister, and mother" (Matt. 12:48, 50).

St. Joseph the craftsman, as a model and as a patron, must enter the world of work once again, today treacherously dominated by the antichrist, by means of ideologies inspired by the latter, oscillating between unbridled capitalism and inhuman communism. From a society "founded on work" (art. 1 of the Italian Constitution), we must return to a society founded on Christ, that is, on the One who sanctifies human work, placing material progress at the service of man's true good, which is not the abundance of earthly goods but the wealth of virtue, to which the work of St. Joseph testifies.

Fr. Serafino's book, at once rigorous and pious, is part of the Holy Spirit's uplifting motion, leading the minds and hearts of those consecrated to the Immaculate to ponder the sublime holiness and singular prerogatives of St. Joseph, her most chaste spouse and virginal father of Jesus. May this precious work contribute to the Josephine devotion of the People of God, to the imitation of his exceptional virtues, and to the development of dogmatic Josephology, thus paving the way for an authoritative intervention of the Supreme Magisterium on this matter.

—Fr. Alessandro M. Apollonio

"De Joseph numquam satis"

The image of St. Joseph presented by this painting, portraying the dream in which the mystery of the Incarnation is revealed to him, harmonizes with the image we wish to impress upon our readers: we are presented with a youthful and vigorous Joseph, to whom Mary has been betrothed. Though they do not yet live together, she is found to be with child through the Holy Spirit. Joseph, neither understanding the mystery nor doubting the innocence of his spouse, silently endures a spiritual sorrow, signified by his furrowed brow, unalleviated by a momentary physical respite. The mystery has remained shrouded in darkness until this moment when, in the silence of the night, the angelic messenger appears, a ray of light pouring from his mouth as he illuminates the mind of Joseph: "Do not fear to take Mary as your wife, for that which is conceived in her is of the Holy Spirit" (Matt. 1:20). The angel gestures both toward Heaven and toward Mary, who has paused in her *lectio divina*, awestruck by this heavenly intervention, her hands crossed in a gesture of gratitude that the heart of her be-loved will now be consoled by the revelation of the mystery hidden within her womb. Joseph will now witness the fulfillment of the prophecy of Isaiah, that a virgin would conceive and give birth to a son named Emmanuel, "God-with-us" (Isa. 7:14).

Joseph awakes from his sleep and promptly obeys the command of the angel of the Lord. His sandals, placed conspicuously in the foreground, suggest both the reverent removal of one's shoes when treading holy ground, sanctified by the divine presence in the word of the angel and in the womb of Mary, along with his readiness for action, as the sleeping saint is ready to spring to his feet, expressing his *fiat* to the divine command not by word but by deed. The silent watchfulness of his heart and his prompt obedience to the divine will manifest his purity of soul and body. Joseph, having been given in marriage to the Ever-Virgin, has undoubtedly been granted the graces necessary for mirroring her virtues, especially her perfect purity and holy virginity. Indeed, Joseph surpasses in sanctity all the saints, excepting his holy spouse, so that we may apply to him the Marian adage: "De Joseph numquam satis," of Joseph we can never say enough. It is in this spirit of Josephine piety that we offer the following reflections as a song of praise to this saint who, after the Blessed Virgin, is unequaled in holiness.

The reader will certainly be wondering why there is a need for yet another book on St. Joseph. Unfortunately, the period following the Second Vatican Council has been characterized by a sort of "Josephine winter," which has stricken and benumbed theology and spirituality, similar to the ongoing "Mariological winter." The figure of St. Joseph has been enveloped by a sort of theological fog, as the late Mariologist Stefano de Fiores once said. Yet, while Mariology has been growing, despite the persistence of a certain minimalism, and is being enriched with new collections of studies, chairs at universities, and numerous publications, this has not been the case for Josephology. However, we can nevertheless note some very encouraging facts in recent years. One significant event that fostered a revival of Josephine spirituality and studies on the holy Carpenter of Nazareth was certainly offered by the Year of St. Joseph, proclaimed by Pope Francis on December 8, 2020. And we cannot fail to mention the tireless work of Fr. Tarcisio Stramare (1928–2020), a profound connoisseur and promoter of Josephine theology, who truly was a *unicum* in the theological-exegetical universe of the last sixty years concerning this theological field. Other recent works, which the reader will find in the bibliography, also bode well for a newfound interest in Josephology. This contribution of ours wishes to contribute to this renewed attempt to make known this unparalleled saint, Joseph of Nazareth, whose greatness is such that an immense quantity of books, articles, and conferences would never suffice to depict it adequately. May the *protodulia* due to him—a primary and special veneration among all the saints—thus become not only a fact known to theologians or present in theological distinctions but also the experience of the faithful, in view of a true renewal of Christian life.

Allow me to make a brief personal aside. My birth and baptismal name is Joseph, inherited from my paternal grandfather on account of an ancient tradition which is widespread in southern Italy, according to which the first male grandchild is named after his grandfather. I was very fortunate. My grandfather Joseph, to whom this book is dedicated, and whose soul I commend to the Lord, was so proud that I bore his name, a name of blessing and grace. Then providence willed that I enter the religious life at a very young age and that I follow the Franciscan tradition of changing my name and adopting a new one. I chose Serafino Maria. You can imagine my grandfather's wrath. Insult was added to injury by his not only having to suffer the "loss" of his grandson but also of his name. He took it quite badly at first. Even my novice master, Fr. Rosario M. Daniello, F.I. (may the Lord welcome him by His side) was not very happy with my choice. He told me I shouldn't change my name for anything in the world: it was far too important. But he left me free to choose. His preoccupation, however, has always remained with me as a reproach, a benevolent admonishment to not forget St. Joseph. I cannot conceal the fact that with the passing of years I have often had second thoughts about my choice to take a new name. It has seemed to me at times that I had wronged the great Joseph of Nazareth, even if such had not been my intention. So, I made a pact with him. I told him that to "repair" my choice, a rather instinctive and youthful way of wanting to start afresh, I would do everything I could to spread his devotion by making him known as best as I was able, through my preaching and writing. I started to write something, especially for the month of March and then, finally, I decided to publish a little book in honor of my Joseph, whose name I still conserve in my heart and in my life, in addition to the religious one. I now put this book into the hands of the reader as a hymn of praise to this saint who, after the Most Holy Virgin, has no equal.

Dante Alighieri's words express in a sublime way the tenacity and zeal inherent in my new publication in honor of St. Joseph:

> But since God willeth that in thee shine forth
> Such grace of his, I'll not be chary with thee.[2]

I will not be sparing in words, dear Joseph. Know that I am your humble servant. I will do my utmost to be a humble voice among many who have praised such a great grace given to you, and to ensure that it will be better known and, above all, imitated.

---

[2] Dante, *Purgatory*, canto 14; verse translation by Henry Wadsworth Longfellow.

To know St. Joseph is to see his presence *in mysterio* already in the Old Covenant. He is prefigured, in fact, by important Old Testament patriarchs. In addition to the figure with whom he is most typically associated, Joseph who, having been sold by his brothers, providentially became prime minister of Egypt thereafter, the great and humble Carpenter of Nazareth is also quite recognizable in other people who have marked the history of Israel, such as Noah, Abraham, and Moses. Let us dwell on these three. Noah builds the ark so that his family may be saved, and with his family, every animal and bird of the air in pairs, male and female (see Gen. 7–9). Through the salvation offered by means of the ark, Noah's family, saved from the waters of the flood that had covered the earth for forty days and forty nights, becomes in turn salvific, repopulating the world in accordance with God's original command: "Be fruitful and multiply." How can we fail to see in this family an image of the Holy Family of Nazareth, saved by Joseph so that it might become the savior of humanity, by the repopulating of the world after its devastation due to sin?

The ark, a figure of the Church that saves us by means of the waters of Baptism, is the place of salvation entrusted to Joseph, patron of the universal Church, so that through his soteriological work in favor of Jesus and His mother, the whole world might thus be saved, through the celebrating of the true sacrifice of salvation. The Father is pleased with this one true holocaust, breathes in its fragrance, and promises never to destroy the earth again (Gen. 8:20–21). The destruction occurred once and for all in the death of the Son on the Cross.

Then there is Abram, the father of a multitude of men as vast as the stars of the firmament (see Gen. 15:5). Abram believes, leaves his land, and heads toward a land that the Lord will show him. A famine arises, obliging him to go to Egypt, which he eventually departs from, going up to the Negeb and settling at the Oaks of Mamre, near Hebron. Abram then becomes Abraham and, through the miraculous gift of his son Isaac, becomes "father of a multitude of nations" (Gen. 17:4). Abraham obeys God's will in every situation, even when very painful, such as the request to sacrifice his son Isaac, who had been given to him in a miraculous way by God. He hopes against all hope. He adores God and entrusts himself to Him; he knows that it will be He who will procure the Lamb for the sacrifice. "God will provide himself the lamb for a burnt offering, my son" (Gen. 22:8), Abraham had said in reply to Isaac. Salvation does not come from the sacrifice of Isaac but from the unique true holocaust offered by Jesus. If Isaac then prefigures Jesus, Abraham cannot fail to prefigure Joseph and Mary, his spouse.

Salvation will not be the fruit of painful human labor but a divine intervention by means of the necessary cooperation of our new Abraham. It is Joseph who guides Jesus day after day toward His final offering. He seeks refuge in Egypt, but then he will leave Egypt and settle in the Land of God because salvation comes from Jerusalem and the Jews. It will be Joseph who will tell Jesus as a child, then as an adolescent, and finally as an adult, after introducing Him, after the silent life of Nazareth, into the mystery of His public life, that it is the Father in Heaven who has provided in His own Son the Lamb for the burnt offering. Joseph prepares the Son for that moment. He lays Him on the altar, which is his heart, as he did at His birth in Bethlehem in a poor manger. He envelops Him in his love and thus offers Him to the world.

Finally, there is Moses, the one who speaks with God "face to face" (Exod. 33:11). Never since has there arisen in Israel the likes of him (Deut. 34:10), although he does not see the face of God but only His back. For the Lord said unto him,

> Behold, there is a place by me where you shall stand upon the rock; and while my glory passes by I will put you in a cleft of the rock, and I will cover you with my hand until I have passed by; then I will take away my hand, and you shall see my back; but my face shall not be seen. (Exod. 33:21–23)

Moses does not see the face of God because God has not yet revealed His face in His son, in Him who knows the Father because He is always turned toward Him: He is in His womb (see John 1:18). In the Son, God reveals Himself, He makes Himself "seen." The Word takes human flesh and makes Himself heard, seen, touched. If John, in fact, can rightly exclaim that he has heard, seen, and touched the Word made flesh, the "word of life" (1 John 1:1), how much more did Joseph of Nazareth, even before the beloved disciple could prepare his senses and "taste" the presence of the Lord among us? Joseph sees Jesus, touches Him, listens to Him, and speaks to Him. He talks face-to-face with God. What was not permitted for Moses is granted to Joseph. He is chosen as the father of the Word and also as the prophet of the Word, His protector and His herald who proclaims Jesus to the world.

Moreover, Joseph in Christ is made a participant in his three-fold *munus* as king, prophet, and priest: king because he enables Christ to reign, so as to reign with Him; prophet, as already mentioned, in that he is the herald of Christ, his word spoken in time, which, however, like the eternal Word, remains in silence; and priest, as he participates in the sacrifice of Christ in a unique way, throughout the unfolding of the Redemption, that is, when that sacrifice was being formed day after day, until the final day without sunset.

In this essay, alongside more habitual themes, we will try to highlight some little-studied but very central aspects of Josephology. In particular, we will examine the participation of St. Joseph in the priesthood of Christ, a theme that remains enveloped in a penumbra, and which requires theological clarification. In our opinion, Joseph's is a unique and exemplary participation, subordinate to that of Mary his spouse, but more excellent and higher than priestly participation in the Church, both in the ministerial priesthood and in the common priesthood. By virtue of his participation in the mystery of the order of hypostatic union, *mediately*, that is, indirectly with respect to Mary's immediate, or direct, participation, Joseph *through* Mary plays a central priestly role in the accomplishment of the Redemption, so as to configure him as a very special cooperator in the Redemption and therefore the sole co-redeemer after Mary. We will thus try to define this unique priesthood of St. Joseph, after reflecting on his co-redemptive participation in our salvation. Therefore, his being a spouse, as some Fathers say, will also be a prefiguration of the Bridegroom-Christ in relation to His Bride-Church, a spousal-salvific role recalling the figure of Joseph of Egypt as a backdrop.

There's more. As we shall see in the following pages, St. Joseph has a relationship of special typicality even with regard to the apostles, with respect to whom he is placed on a higher level, as his is superior to that of all the other saints, including the Precursor. St. Hilary of Poitiers (ca. 310–367), in his commentary on the Gospel of Matthew (2:1), already highlighted this relationship of typicality. Joseph *anticipates*, according to him, the apostolic ministry which consists in spreading the presence and action of

Christ. Here is what he writes, interweaving the life of St. Joseph with that of the apostles:

> Joseph provides an image of the apostles (*apostolorum habet speciem*), to whom Christ was entrusted for dissemination far and wide (*Christus circumferendus*). These men were commanded to preach to the Jews, because even as Herod was being overtaken by death, his people were becoming lost as to the meaning of the Lord's Passion. The apostles had been sent to the "lost sheep of the house of Israel," but because the domination of a hereditary infidelity persisted, they were afraid and drew back. Joseph was warned in a dream, by which we understand how the gift of the Holy Spirit was directed to the pagans. The apostles now have announced life and salvation for the pagans, introducing them to Christ, who was sent to the Jews.

This quote is simply to give the reader a mere glimpse of a saint who, after the Blessed Virgin Mary, is the greatest. He surpasses in excellence and holiness—by reason of his unique mission—all the saints, apostles, martyrs, the choir of virgins, and even the angelic choirs, precisely like the Virgin Mary his spouse, to whom alone he is subordinate. It is no exaggeration, then, if we repeat the famous Marian adage, now applying it to our saint: "De Joseph numquam satis," of Joseph we can never say enough. Hence the reason for this book. We will attempt to shed light on some features of the life and mission of the holy craftsman of Nazareth; we will try to do this in a new way and with a new emphasis. In this essay we will analyze three key characteristic features: the man, the spouse, and the father, all of which lead to the soteriological mystery by virtue of the unique mission entrusted to Joseph by the Father, this mission being enriched by his eternal predestination and his singular grace. Everything then converges in the fact of Joseph as being the exemplary *type* of consecration to Mary.

He is the one in whom everything begins *through* Mary and everything is fulfilled *in* Jesus. He is the true icon of devotion to Mary and of consecration to her. Through Mary, Joseph came into contact with the mystery of the Son of God; he becomes the father of Jesus by imposing on Him His name and thus participates in a unique way in the salvific plan as *minister* of the mysteries of the hidden life of Jesus. The marriage with Mary is also the way to a profound mystical union with the Mother of God, woven of the highest love, service, and effective collaboration, *a type* of union of every soul with the Virgin Mary. Like John the Evangelist, but first and in a more perfect way, Joseph received Mary not so much or only into his house as among his most precious things. He welcomed her into his soul, his life, by becoming her unlimited property. It is also in this—especially in this—that Joseph is the *exemplum* to imitate. He tells us, with all the other saints: *ad Jesum per Mariam.* If we go to Jesus through Mary, we do precisely what Joseph did, and we do so with Joseph.

Through him, without any doubt, we will also be able to rediscover the figure of the father, so indispensable to the contemporary world, as well as the pearl of virginity and of chastity, taboos in a society that has set God aside and that now, having been hollowed out, finds itself helpless in the face of the evil of impurity that has spread far and wide, on all sides, and in every shape and form. We find ourselves in an orphaned society, engulfed in impurity: two dominant notes that invite us now more than ever to go to Joseph, to treasure his presence in the Church and in Christian piety.

In the following pages, we will interpret the Josephine mystery with the theological-sapiential help of the Fathers of the

Church and the saints. In the Fathers, in particular, Joseph is presented principally as guardian of or witness to the virginity of Mary, himself also being a virgin, and, as the father of the Savior, minister of the divine economy. We find in them a treasure trove of teachings. Our effort will be to simplify the Josephine theological doctrines and to make them as far as possible a way to deepen our catechetical-spiritual understanding of the figure of the Nazarene Craftsman. Our selection will therefore be based on this theological-spiritual aim. The book as a whole aims to be an example of a theology that becomes spirituality, with theology gradually tending toward spirituality as to its most perfect end, and of a theological spirituality that is open to prayer to him who is destined, with Mary and through Mary, to conform us to her son, Jesus. "Ite ad Ioseph," "Go to Joseph" is the imperative that we would like to echo from these pages in the hearts and minds of our readers. *Turn to Joseph*, dear reader, know him more to love and venerate him more. It is my wish that he will become, for you as well, your special patron saint.

Part 1

The Man, the Spouse, and the Father

Before delving into doctrinal considerations about Joseph as just man, holy spouse, and providential father, let us contemplate this beautiful portrayal of our saint and endeavour to see him through the gaze of Our Lady. Fr. Frederick Faber can help us do so:

> Joseph was to Mary the shadow of the Eternal Father, the representative of her Heavenly Spouse, the Holy Ghost. In him she saw with awful clearness and most reverential tenderness two Persons of the Most Holy Trinity. When she saw Jesus in his arms, it was a mystery to her too deep for words. Tears only could express it.[3]

She who is the heavenly Illuminatrix gazed upon all the wondrous world and perceived therein the sign of the triune God, and never more so than when contemplating holy Joseph. If we could see with Mary's eyes, we would perceive, as in this painting, hovering over her earthly spouse, the dove of the Holy Ghost, her unearthly Spouse, whose celestial luminescence is shared by the flesh of the Infant Christ and is reflected upon the face of Joseph. Our gaze, illumined by her flawless faith, would see

---

[3] Frederick Faber, D.D., *At the Foot of the Cross: Or, The Sorrows of Mary*, 4th ed. (London: Thomas Richardson, 1872), 139.

in the Infant the Son of God, and in Joseph the figure of His heavenly Father; in Joseph's benevolent watchfulness over the Child in his arms, we would discern the very image of the divine providence of the Eternal Father. Then our eyes would follow Our Lady's gaze which, from Joseph, would rest upon her son, thus completing the trinitarian image, illumining our mind's eye with the mystery of the thrice-holy Godhead. Her unsurpassable reverence would touch our hearts, moistening our eyes with her tears of sheer felicity.

Then the lucent-eyed Virgin would enlighten our minds, enabling us to delve more deeply into the mystery. We would grasp that, just as the Son is generated in eternity by the Father, and begotten in time by the Holy Spirit, so likewise He is, in a sense, generated spiritually and begotten virginally by Joseph by virtue of his spiritual paternity and his virginal sponsality. Through his virginal love, symbolized by the lily he holds in his hand, he treasures and safeguards the mystery of Christ's divinity. The Word, although forever with the Father beyond all time, confides His holy humanity in time to the care of His earthly father. Joseph's chaste Heart is like a virginal cradle for the Christ Child, guarding the mystery of the Redemption and, above all, adoring the sacred mystery. Enlightened by Mary, we would understand that, just as God the Father eternally utters the Word, so likewise Joseph, by giving Jesus His name, echoes this eternal utterance. "Nomen est omen": as the name signifies the essence of the thing named, so Joseph, by naming Jesus, designates Him as Savior, thereby inaugurating His redemptive mission as well as his own co-redemptive mission.

Illuminated thus by the gaze of our Blessed Mother, our eyes would be aglow with the golden sheen of the garment enveloping Joseph, symbolizing the divine light of Christ with which his whole being was imbued, and our hearts would sing:

> In glorious Holy Joseph did Our Lady see
> The mirror image of the Holy Trinity.
> In all humility, he served God faithfully,
> So blessed may he be, for all eternity!

St. Joseph is the greatest saint after the Blessed Virgin Mary. The Fathers of the Church, the saints, and the Magisterium bear witness to this. All unanimously sing his greatness, portray his glories as intertwined with his unspeakable sorrows, and invite us to invoke his holy name, which, after that of Jesus and Mary, is the name of salvation, of intercession, and of grace. As Pope Francis reminds us in his apostolic letter *Patris corde* (December 8, 2020), on the occasion of the 150th anniversary of the declaration of St. Joseph as patron of the universal Church, "After Mary, Mother of God, no saint occupies as much space in the papal Magisterium as Joseph, her spouse" (introduction). Never could enough be said of him for his unique role in the history of salvation as admirable spouse and father, as guardian of the mysteries of God and faithful executor of the will of the Father in Heaven.

The greatness of St. Joseph is well described by St. John Henry Newman, who in the *Meditations for the Triduum of St. Joseph* writes that:

> He was the true and worthy Spouse of Mary, supplying in a visible manner the place of Mary's Invisible Spouse, the Holy Ghost. He was a virgin, and his virginity was the faithful mirror of the virginity of Mary. He was the Cherub, placed to guard the new terrestrial Paradise from the intrusion of every foe.... He is Holy Joseph, because according to the opinion of a great number of doctors, he, as well as St. John Baptist, was sanctified even before he was born. He is Holy Joseph, because his office, of being

spouse and protector of Mary, specially demanded sanctity. He is Holy Joseph, because no other saint but he lived in such and so long intimacy and familiarity with the source of all holiness, Jesus, God incarnate, and Mary, the holiest of creatures.[4]

The name "Joseph" comes from the Hebrew root *yasaf* which means "to add," "to increase." We find a reference to this in the book of Genesis when God grants Rachel her first son, Joseph, the penultimate of Jacob's twelve sons. Rachel, although a spouse more beloved than Leah, had remained sterile. When she finally gives birth, she exclaims: "God has taken away my reproach," and "May the Lord add to me another son!" (Gen. 30:22–24). It is interesting to note that the name Joseph, like that of the other patriarchs, is not taken from a deity or a hero but is the expression of a supplication raised to God. Then there is another explanation of the name "Joseph," according to the blessing formula with which Jacob blessed his twelve sons, the tribes of Israel. Joseph is the only one blessed with this eloquent formula:

> By the God of your father who will help you,
> by God Almighty who will bless you,
> with blessings of heaven above,
> blessings of the deep that couches beneath,
> blessings of the breasts and of the womb.
> The blessings of your father
> are mighty beyond the blessings of the eternal
> mountains,
> the bounties of the everlasting hills;

---

[4] John Henry Newman, *A Triduum to St. Joseph*, in *Prayers, Verses and Devotions* (San Francisco: Ignatius Press, 2019), 320–322.

may they be on the head of Joseph,
> and on the brow of him who was separate from his
> brothers. (Gen. 49:25–26)

In the first Joseph, son of Jacob, we can already glimpse our Joseph, who has been blessed "with blessings of heaven above." Bl. Pius IX, after proclaiming, on December 8, 1870, St. Joseph Patron of the Church (with the decree *Quemadmodum Deus*), thus accepting the request of the First Vatican Council, a year later promulgated the apostolic letter *Inclytum patriarcham*. In this letter he affirmed the superiority of St. Joseph over all the other saints. This superiority is due to the fact that he was chosen with Christ and Mary to take part in the work of the Incarnation and Redemption, as can be deduced from the Gospel accounts in which he is defined as Mary's spouse and as the father, the guardian, of the incarnate Word. These considerations allow us to enter into the profound mystery that is hidden in the person and life of St. Joseph.

On August 15, 1889, Leo XIII published an encyclical letter, entitled *Quamquam pluries*, on devotion to St. Joseph. Referring to what had been done by his predecessor, who had declared our saint to be the patron of the Church, he provides a rich theological explanation of the fittingness of this title, anchoring it to two unsurpassable privileges that make Joseph a unique saint, above all others, after Jesus and Mary: that of being the spouse of Mary and the foster father of Jesus. Here is an illuminating passage from this encyclical:

> The special motives for which St. Joseph has been proclaimed Patron of the Church, and from which the Church looks for singular benefit from his patronage and protection, are that Joseph was the spouse of Mary

and that he was reputed the Father of Jesus Christ. From these sources have sprung his dignity, his holiness, his glory. In truth, the dignity of the Mother of God is so lofty that naught created can rank above it. But as Joseph has been united to the Blessed Virgin by the ties of marriage, it may not be doubted that he approached nearer than any to the eminent dignity by which the Mother of God surpasses so nobly all created natures. For marriage is the most intimate of all unions which from its essence imparts a community of gifts between those that by it are joined together. Thus in giving Joseph the Blessed Virgin as spouse, God appointed him to be not only her life's companion, the witness of her maidenhood, the protector of her honour, but also, by virtue of the conjugal tie, a participator in her sublime dignity. (no. 3)

John Paul II in his most important Josephine document, *Redemptoris custos*, published on August 15, 1989, referring to the magisterium of his predecessors, presents St. Joseph as "depositary of the mystery of God" (no. 15), to the point that his faith is one with the faith of Mary. Being Mary's spouse means above all participating in her faith. He receives everything from the Mother of God and, in some way, in like manner to the Mother of God, to the degree befitting to him. John Paul II writes:

One can say that what Joseph did united him in an altogether special way to the faith of Mary. He accepted as truth coming from God the very thing that she had already accepted at the Annunciation.... Therefore he became a unique guardian of the mystery "hidden for ages in God" (Eph 3:9), as did Mary, in that decisive moment which St. Paul calls "the fullness of time," when "God sent forth his Son, born of woman … to redeem those who were under the law, so that we might receive adoption as sons" (Gal 4:4–5). … Together with Mary, Joseph is the first guardian of this divine mystery. Together with Mary, and in relation to Mary, he shares in this final phase of God's self-revelation in Christ and he does so from the very beginning. (nos. 4–5)

Everything in Joseph's life is intertwined with that of Mary. The Virgin's *fiat* at the Annunciation of the angel finds its counterpart in the prompt obedience of the holy carpenter in fulfilling God's will. That "Do not be afraid" addressed to Mary by the archangel Gabriel (Luke 1:30), with which the Virgin was reassured that she would become a mother without ceasing to be a virgin consecrated to God, echoes strongly in the "Do not fear" addressed to Joseph (Matt. 1:20). He, too, is invited by the angel—perhaps Gabriel himself—to turn his gaze to the perpetual virginity of Mary, his spouse; a virginity that Joseph had deep down also chosen for himself, from the beginning, and as a spousal gift, with Mary. "Do not be afraid to take Mary with you," the angel suggests, "because what is in you has always remained in her too." Joseph had no doubts, but now he has the heavenly guarantee that his spouse is not only both virgin and mother but is also the true Ark of the Covenant, the tabernacle of the Most High. To borrow a phrase from St. Augustine, Joseph is all the more spouse that he is all the more chaste. He will be a father by gently approaching that holy Ark without touching her. He will be one of the two cherubim, together with a heavenly one, in loving vigilance at one side of the propitiatory; indeed, he will be the true propitiatory of pure gold placed on the Ark of the Covenant, sealing it and thus protecting it from any extraneous contact. St. Jacob of Sarug (ca. 451–521), a Syriac monk and great poet with a flowery style, defines Joseph as a "cherub of flesh," a craftsman who acts as minister to the Craftsman of the world. Here is his text:

> Joseph led the faithful one, who came unto him, and the Virgin dwelt with this saint in perfect chastity. He serves, loves, honours her and rejoices in her, exalting and praising her ministry in a holy manner. Holy is his body, pure his heart, chaste his thoughts. A cherub of flesh, he became a craftsman for the Craftsman of the world, and with integrity he accepted this ministry with perfect purity. (*Homily on the Nativity of the Lord*, prose translation of vv. 768–770)

Moreover, through Mary, this holy craftsman is introduced into the house of God, into the very heart of God, becoming His father and always acting "with a father's heart: that is how Joseph loved Jesus" (*Patris corde*, introduction). Mary unites Joseph with Jesus and unites Jesus, through Joseph's intercession, with all of us. Let us venture forth, then, with decisive steps and with an open heart, into the contemplation of this great saint of whom we can never say enough. As to Mary, so likewise to her saintly spouse we can apply the well-known adage: "De Joseph numquam satis"—of Joseph one can never be satiated, literally; all that can be said of him will never be said, as indeed is also the case of his most holy spouse.

Why is St. Joseph so great? asks Fr. Stefano M. Manelli, in his valuable book for the month of March in honor of our saint. His response sets the tone for our itinerary when he says that

> St. Joseph's mission was an exceptional mission, *unique in the world!* His was a divine mission so exceptional that,

concretely, it surpassed not only the order of human nature, but also that of the angelic nature and also, finally, the very order of grace that St. John the Baptist had in preparing the way for the Lord, that of the apostles in evangelizing for the salvation and sanctification of souls, and that of the founders of religious orders and institutes.[5]

5 Stefano M. Manelli, *Il mese di San Giuseppe: Meditazioni per ogni giorno del mese di marzo* (Frigento, Italy: Casa Mariana Editrice, 2018), 18.

Chapter 1

The Just Man

Let us begin by considering St. Joseph as a just and righteous man before reflecting on him as spouse of Mary and virginal father of Jesus. The latter are indeed two prerogatives that, in a unique way, place Joseph of Nazareth, the humble carpenter, in the mystery of God, thus making him a close participant in the Redemption. St. Joseph is chosen by God as guardian of His mysteries in time: Jesus and Mary. The unique predilection of the Father is directed toward him, designating him as father of His Son and spouse of His daughter. God's treasures are placed into his hands and entrusted to his care. He is the treasurer of the house of God. And yet an aura of silence and deep humility surrounds him. The great things of God are enveloped in humility, in hiddenness. They are great precisely to the extent that they are insignificant in the eyes of men. It is by humbling oneself that one becomes great. Is this not the most apparent paradox of the gospel? The humble Carpenter of Nazareth embodies this in his life. Joseph is "added by God" to His family so that the features of a fatherhood and a sponsality imbued with humble greatness and wise smallness may be sketched out in his person.

St. Joseph is a figure who fascinates due to the greatness of his vocation that is hidden between the lines of sparsely recounted familial events, interwoven with tribulations and thorns. However, if one delves deeply, through careful contemplation of what little information we have of him, one can perceive a majestic figure. Matthew likes to designate St. Joseph as the "just man." It is an attribute that the evangelist applies to him in passing, to explain the reason for his prudent decision in the face of the conception of his wife whom he firmly recognized as being holy and inhabited by a mystery. Faced with this mystery, Joseph, fearing to interfere with God's will, withdraws. It is characteristic of humble people to step aside to make room for God. Joseph, who loved hiddenness and above all who loved the hidden God, desired to conceal himself to make room for Him in the life of his spouse. "Her husband Joseph," says the evangelist, "being a just man and unwilling to put her to shame, resolved to send her away quietly" (Matt. 1:19).

It is very probable that the evangelist drew this very intimate information from Joseph's family, that is, from the most profound intimacy of Nazareth, without needing to have recourse to numerous exegetical acrobatics, such as a retrospective reflection on the part of the hagiographer, starting from the facts of the Lord's public life, ultimately to then call into question the historicity of this very information.

Joseph was therefore "just," imbued with a justice that rendered him akin to the ancient patriarchs, a man of God, a man of faith and obedience to the will of God. Joseph believed without wavering in the God of the covenant. He offered his life to Him and, as a pious Israelite, meditated on the Word of the Lord day and night. With the Psalmist, in the secret of his inner chamber, he addressed this prayer to God:

> Give me understanding, that I may keep thy law
>   and observe it with my whole heart.

Lead me in the path of your commandments,
for I delight in it. (Ps. 119:34–35)

The Patriarch Abraham, Figure of St. Joseph

A very beautiful prefiguration of St. Joseph, a righteous man *par excellence*, who truly hopes against hope (see Rom. 4:18), can be found, as we have seen, in the patriarch Abraham. Just as Abraham had believed, without ever faltering in his faith (Rom. 4:19), so our new patriarch—in the etymological sense of "first father"—firmly believes in God, entrusts himself to His will, and obeys. While Joseph was thinking in his heart that he would depart from his spouse whom he perceived to be enveloped in a golden mystery, an angel of the Lord appeared to him and said to him: "Joseph, son of David, do not be afraid to take Mary your wife, for that which is conceived in her is of the Holy Spirit" (Matt. 1:20). Joseph the just needs nothing else. Though he, too, is now enveloped in mystery, when an angel speaks to him and announces a supernatural conception of his spouse by the power of the Holy Spirit, he understands and believes. He believes with the obedience of faith.

In this we can clearly see the justice of St. Joseph, his holiness: he is no stranger to mystery, he does not remain indecisive even for an instant when faced with that utterly astonishing scenario. Joseph was a man of prayer, accustomed to dialoguing with God. We can certainly think that Joseph was awaiting in a prayerful way the coming of the Messiah. He knew the Scriptures perfectly, and with the prophets, he raised his voice heavenward and faithfully awaited the propitious moment when the Heavens would be torn open so that the Savior might descend (see Isa. 64:1). Certainly, in his most profound humility, he never thought that he would be chosen to become the father of the Messiah, yet his desire to see salvation fulfilled and grace flourish among men had been growing day by day.

Joseph is also accustomed to transcending the events of life and interpreting them in the light of the Faith and of the will of Yahweh. Finally, awakening from his slumber, as if aroused from an intimate conversation with the Most High, "he did as the angel of the Lord commanded him; he took his wife, but knew her not until she had borne a son; and he called his name Jesus" (Matt. 1:24-25). Then, once again, an angel of the Lord appeared in a dream to Joseph and ordered him to flee to Egypt because of Herod's violent persecution. Joseph, as the new Abraham, leaves his land, takes his dearest treasures, and flees to Egypt. He sets off into the unknown: Would he be able to find a house, a job? Joseph was a holy man. He entrusts himself to God's will and obeys. God will provide: He will be there. The exile will soon end, and Joseph, always obeying the voice of the angel, will return to his land. He will give back to that blessed land its sun, its salt.

Just as Abraham, of whom God had asked his only son—although knowing, however, that God can bring forth children even from stones (see Matt. 3:9)—had not hesitated to obey His will, likewise does Joseph accept the will of the Father who gives him His son and asks him to guard Him, raise Him, and educate Him (in the etymological sense of "leading him") for the great day of bloody immolation. Although he did not himself offer the Son at the sublime moment of Calvary—which Jesus' mother would do, though he had done so *in signo* at the presentation of Jesus in the temple—Joseph had disposed everything so that his son could prepare Himself throughout His years of human growth for the culminating moment of His earthly life: the sacrifice of the Cross. Just as Jesus is the true Isaac, so Joseph of Nazareth—like his spouse Mary—is the true Abraham. St. Joseph, who had welcomed the Son of God and had safeguarded Him, was aware that this Son had to do the Father's will (see Luke 2:49). Obedient, he hands Him back in sacrifice with all his paternal love and, silently, leaves the scene; he falls asleep in God to then be awakened by the Son victorious over sin and death. Joseph was the first just man to whom Christ held out His hand. Few but truly sublime features thus sculpt a very lofty figure of holiness: Joseph of Nazareth, "the just man," a saint who truly spoke "face-to-face" with God, as Moses had done, but much more so than him and in a personal way.

Chapter 2

The Holy Spouse

Nothing less than a truly just man, the most righteous of men, would be fitting in order to be a worthy spouse of the Blessed Virgin. St. Joseph was indeed the most holy spouse of Mary and their marriage was a true marriage. From the Gospel accounts of Luke (1:27) and Matthew (1:16, 18–21) we can deduce that at the time of the Annunciation, Mary had already been betrothed to Joseph, although they did not yet live together. The Hebrew marriage took place in two stages: the official engagement in which the two were already legally espoused and which could last up to a year, then the actual wedding which consisted in the husband's taking of his spouse with him in cohabitation.

St. Augustine reacts against the Pelagian Julian, bishop of Eclanum, who denied the veracity of the marriage between Mary and Joseph on the grounds that it had not been consummated. St. Augustine, in response to Julian, places its essence not in the union of bodies but in the union of souls, the latter taking place with consent (*fide copulatus*). As the *Code of Canon Law* also states, the act that constitutes marriage is the consent of the engaged (can. 1057, § 1), that is, a clear manifestation of the will of both to take one another as husband and wife. In the words of the *Code*, "Matrimonial consent is an act of the will by which a man and a woman mutually give and accept each other through an irrevocable covenant in order to establish marriage" (can. 1057, § 2). John Paul II, in *Redemptoris custos* (no. 7) testifies that "Analyzing the nature of marriage, both St. Augustine and St. Thomas always identify it with an 'indivisible union of souls,' a 'union of hearts,' with 'consent.' These elements are found in an exemplary manner in the marriage of Mary and Joseph." It is very beautiful to reflect on marriage as a union of hearts and souls. The truth of its essence is spiritual and not carnal. Mary and Joseph incarnated this essence in the most sublime way and therefore serve as a model for all married people.

Let us quote at greater length the great St. Augustine who, in several of his works, as Pope John Paul II reminded us, defends the truth of the marriage between Mary and Joseph. In the *Contra Faustum*, St. Augustine reminds us that Joseph is called Mary's husband in that he possessed her as his spouse chastely, "not through carnal knowledge but through affection, not through the union of bodies but through that, far more precious, of souls" (23:8).

Moreover, highlighting what at first glance could cause dissonance, the Davidic genealogy of Jesus through Joseph, Mary's spouse, and the fact that Joseph did not generate Jesus according to the flesh, Augustine asks, in the same work just cited, the following question:

> Why, then, should a follower of the Gospel be disconcerted by the fact that Christ, born of the virgin Mary without any carnal union with Joseph, is nevertheless called the son of David, even though the evangelist Matthew conducts his genealogy not as far as Mary, but as far as Joseph? (23:8)

He responds by arguing that

> Joseph, by virtue of manly dignity, should not be separated
> from the sequence of those generations, so that by this he
> would not seem to be separated from the woman to whom
> the affection of the soul united him, and that the faithful
> men of Christ should not believe that, in marriage, carnal
> union with one's wife is so important that one is not mar-
> ried without it, but rather that they might comprehend
> that faithful spouses adhere all the more intimately to the
> members of Christ that they have been able to imitate
> Christ's parents. (23:8)

This, then, is the reason for the exemplarity of this holy Josephine marriage. One adheres all the more to the members of
Christ, to His Mystical Body, that one imitates Christ's parents.
Their profound spiritual union is the very type of the union of
the members of Christ with their Head: a union that we can well
define as spousal. Therefore, with Mary and Joseph, in their holy
marriage, we learn to live in a spousal way above all the union with
the Lord in His Body which is the Church, at which Christian
marriage fundamentally aims.

This concept of the paradigmatic value of the marriage of
Mary and Joseph will be taken up by St. Augustine in his work
The Harmony of the Gospels:

> For by this example an illustrious recommendation is
> made to faithful married persons of the principle, that
> even when by common consent they maintain their
> continence, the relation can still remain, and can still be
> called one of wedlock, inasmuch as, although there is no
> connection between the sexes of the body, there is the
> keeping of the affections of the mind. (2, 1, 2)

This marriage with Mary will be for Joseph his official entry into the mystery of God. Joseph unites himself to Mary in marriage and thus finds Jesus, becomes one with Him, to the point of becoming His father. We will return again to this spousal doctrine, which is so very central. For now, it will suffice to have introduced it in its truth and spirituality.

Did Joseph Ever Have a Moment's Doubt About Mary's Integrity?

Let us now address in greater detail the problem of the reaction, or rather the state of mind, of St. Joseph when he learned that his spouse was pregnant. The Gospel of Matthew (1:18–19) presents us with this moment in this way:

> Now the birth of Jesus Christ took place in this way. When his mother Mary had been betrothed to Joseph, before they came together she was found to be with child of the Holy Spirit; and her husband Joseph, being a just man and unwilling to put her to shame [*deigmatisai* = expose her, make of her an example of disgrace], resolved to send her away [*apolûsai* = put her away, free her from the marital obligation] quietly."

At a first reading of the text, the first thought that immediately springs to the reader's mind is that Joseph is in a very difficult situation. He has to make a hard decision: on the one hand, he is perfectly aware of the holiness of his spouse and of her vow of virginity which he had approved, otherwise the marriage would have been invalid, and which he certainly imitated (on this precise aspect we will return later); on the other hand, he is confronted with an astonishing fact which goes beyond the ordinary course of things. His spouse has become pregnant before their coming to live together. He appears to be unaware of the fact that the Holy Spirit is the protagonist of this virginal conception, although the text says that Mary "was found to be with child of the Holy Spirit," as if to underline the fact of her pregnancy as well as its cause. And being just, that is, full of every virtue, and not wanting to expose his spouse to public ridicule in the face of that unexpected situation, Joseph decides to put her away in secret or to leave in secret.

Three Theories on Joseph's State of Knowledge

Since the time of the Fathers of the Church, this text and all its possible implications have been thoroughly investigated. We can summarize in three theories the state of knowledge of St. Joseph at the time of the miraculous Incarnation of the Son of God by the power of the Holy Spirit, already well outlined in the first five centuries:

a. He suspected that Mary had committed adultery.
b. Although he did not suspect adultery, he knew nothing of the miraculous conception, and so he suspended all judgment.
c. The miraculous conception of Mary by the Holy Spirit had already been made known to him. Joseph was afraid to take Mary as his wife because of the magnitude of the miracle wrought in her. So he decides to leave.

St. Justin Martyr (ca. 100–165) thinks that St. Joseph doubted the integrity of Our Lady, believing that she was pregnant because of a relationship with a man and therefore had the intention of putting her away, which he renounced doing after the appearance of the angel (see *Dialogue with Trypho*, 78). St. Ambrose (ca. 340–397), on the other hand, admitting Joseph's ignorance of the mystery, believes this led him to dismiss his spouse while simply suspecting her guilt (*vitium*). After the instruction of the angel, no longer doubting her virginity, he carried out the command (see *Epistle 5*,13). "What prejudice does it do to Mary," he asks, "if Joseph did not understand the mystery of heavenly counsel and thought that she had lost her virginity when he saw her pregnant?" (*De institutione virginis*, 5, 39–40). Even the angels were unaware of the Resurrection. However, Joseph, who is just, does not condemn. He prefers to be accused of clemency for not having denounced, rather than insist on the crime of others, says St. Ambrose (*In Psalmum 118 Expositio*, 7, 24). St. Augustine (354–430) shares his opinion (*Epistle 153*, 4, 9; *Sermo 51*, 6, 9; *Sermo 82*, 7, 10).

St. Jerome (ca. 347–419/420) believes instead that, although Joseph did not suspect his spouse of adultery, but rather trusting in her purity and marveling at what had happened, he enveloped in silence a mystery that he could not rationally explain. He says thusly, in a lapidary way: "Joseph, knowing her chastity and perplexed by what had taken place, conceals in silence the mystery that he did not know about" (*Commentary on the Gospel of Matthew*, 1, 1, v. 19).

In support of his preference for virginity over marriage, Jerome, in his work entitled *On the Perpetual Virginity of Mary: Against Helvidius*, refutes the latter's claim that after Jesus, Our Lady had other children, that the mention of the "brothers and sisters" of Jesus in the Gospels proved precisely this, and that, consequently, the marital state was superior to the virginal state; Jerome, on the contrary, affirms that not only Mary but also Joseph remained in the virginal state: "You say that Mary did not continue a virgin: I claim still more that Joseph himself, on account of Mary (*per*

Mariam), was a virgin, so that from a virginal marriage a virgin son might be born" (19). He affirms that the term "brother" or "sister" of Jesus is not to be understood according to nature (15–16); that marriage, though it can sometimes be a holy patrimony, presents great obstacles to prayer; and that the teaching of Scripture is that the states of virginity and continence are more in conformity with the will of God than that of marriage (20–22).

St. Jerome also points out, against the apocryphal writings, which he calls "delusions," that St. Joseph was young and not old, not a widower but virile and capable of chastity. He was given in marriage to the virgin and could only but follow *in primis* and foremost such a sublime example. Jesus' brothers and sisters are therefore not Joseph's children from a previous marriage but are Jesus' cousins or other relatives (see, among other things, his *Commentary on the Gospel of Matthew*, 2, 12, 49–50).

The position of St. Jerome is also shared by St. Peter Chrysologus (ca. 380–450), the first of the Fathers to use the Marian expressions *Sponsa Dei* and *Sponsa Christi*. Joseph, in uncertainty, finds himself alone before God and entrusts all judgment to Him. Here is a very meaningful passage from his Sermon 145 *De generationi Christi et de Joseph Mariam dimittere volente*, in which the saint reflects on Joseph's soul, which was "throbbing" with pain in front of the event of Mary's conception:

> What was the husband to do in such a case? Was he to accuse her of sin? But he himself was witness of her innocence. Should he publish her fault? But he himself was the guardian of her purity. Was he to press a charge of adultery? But he was the herald of her virginity. What was he to do in such circumstances? He thought of putting her away, since he could neither reveal outside what had

happened, nor keep it inside. He thought of putting her away, and he told it all to God, because he had nothing to tell to men.

Weight is lent to this opinion by another powerful testimony, provided by the Benedictine mystic and servant of God, Mother Maria Cecilia Baij (1694–1766), in her *Life of the Glorious Patriarch St. Joseph*.

The third hypothesis, that Joseph knew of Mary's miraculous conception by the Holy Spirit and felt unworthy to take her as his wife, is supported by a homily attributed to Origen (183–255), *On the Eve of the Nativity of the Lord*. In this text, Origen argues that, by reason of Mary's holiness, Joseph considered himself unfit to live with her, having become aware of the mystery of the Incarnation that was hidden in the womb of his spouse. Joseph, knowing from the Holy Spirit that the pregnancy was from God and considering this mystery to be too great for him to remain by the Virgin's side, would have exclaimed like St. Peter: "Go away from me, Lord, for I am a sinful man!" or like Elizabeth: "And why has this happened to me, that the mother of my Lord comes to me?"

This view that Joseph discovered Mary's pregnancy and its cause is also shared by St. Basil the Great (ca. 330–379), who states that Joseph, fearing to be called the man (*vir*) of such a woman, preferred to put her away secretly. In St. Basil's opinion, Joseph was not indignant toward his spouse, nor had he felt disgust toward her. He solely feared her, being filled with the Holy Spirit (*Homily on the Holy Generation of Christ*, 4).

Finally, this third possibility is also dear to St. Bernard of Clairvaux (1090–1153). In his famous and heartfelt homily *Super Missus est*, that is, on the archangel Gabriel who brings the announcement to Mary, Bernard also wonders why Joseph wanted to repudiate his spouse. The motive was the same as Peter's for distancing the Lord from himself (see Luke 5:8), or as the Roman centurion who says: "Lord, I am not worthy to have you come under my roof" (Matt. 8:8). Similarly:

> Joseph looked on himself as a sinner and as unworthy to entertain one in whom he beheld a superhuman dignity. He beheld with awe in the Virgin-Mother a certain sign of the Divine Presence, and as he could not penetrate the mystery, he wished to put her away (2:14).

Later, however, Bernard returns to the question and instead seems to see a doubt on the part of Joseph. As he was just, he refused to live with a suspicious person, and as he was good, he refrained from exposing her. However, according to him, that doubt was necessary, because in this way Joseph's doubt merited "to be dispelled by Divine intervention" (2:15).

As we can see, the panorama of reflections on that dramatic moment in the life of the holy Nurturer of Jesus are varied and with many nuances. Now, reflecting on these three theories we must immediately say that the first, that of the suspicion of adultery, although shared by eminent Fathers, is not at all acceptable: it lacks a solid foundation. Moreover, it is contrary to the meaning of Matthew's text as a whole, not taking into account above all the fact that, as Joseph is "just" and does not want to publicly repudiate his spouse, he did not consider her guilty of adultery. A prudent and holy man like him would have asked his spouse for an explanation before believing her guilty of a crime so abominable to her, whom he knew to be holy and God-fearing.

As for the second theory, which highlights a suspension of judgment on the part of Joseph, although it is the one that finds the most favor among theologians, it is also open to criticism. In fact, if Joseph is "just" (*dikaios*), how could he have distanced himself from his spouse, abandoning her at such a delicate moment? The strength of this position lies in the fact that Joseph does not know of the virginal conception and therefore, as a just man, prefers to wait for God to give him a sign. Yet it seems that even if Mary had kept silent about the event of the Incarnation, without revealing it to her husband, the latter could still have been informed of it by Mary's relatives, especially after the Visitation, when the signs of pregnancy were already evident. How could it be possible for Elizabeth to recognize Mary as "the mother of my Lord" but for Joseph to still remain unaware? After all, it is unlikely that our saint would have failed to recognize the fulfillment of Isaiah's prophecy (7:14): "Behold, a young woman shall conceive and bear a son," since the expectation of the Messiah in his time was so strong. Therefore, it seems that Joseph learned of the Incarnation of the Son of God in Mary's womb and, filled with fear in the face of such a great mystery, decided to leave.

Thus, we come to the third theory, that of humility in the face of the mystery. Joseph is God-fearing: he knows that God is a jealous God. The angel's words would not be a solution to his doubt but a command that puts order in his fearful uncertainty. "Joseph, son of David, do not fear to take Mary your wife, for that which is conceived in her is of the Holy Spirit" (Matt. 1:20). The "Do not fear" would be the assurance not to leave for reasons of unworthiness. Yet even the latter presents some critical issues. The "for" (*gàr*) seems here to introduce the reason for "Do not fear." It could also be translated as "since" or "because" and thus would indicate the revelation that Joseph finally receives from the angel of the virginal fruit of Mary's womb. In reality, the particle *gàr* of the Gospel of Matthew is used with prodigality, even where the other

Gospels in the parallel passages instead omit it (see, e.g., Matt. 5:46; 9:24; 24:6; 25:29; 26:28; 28:5). But if one reflects more on this theory as a whole, one might even doubt the true humility of St. Joseph. In fact, it must now necessarily be presumed that Joseph had been informed of the virginal conception before the apparition of the angel, if not by Mary herself, as would seem more logical, at least by her relatives. Why, however, if Mary in her profound humility accepted to become the Mother of God, would Joseph instead prefer to renounce his mission? Would it not have been more logical for Mary herself to have encouraged her spouse to place all his trust in God and to accept his fatherhood?

This third position rightly excludes any doubt on the part of Joseph, and it is precisely to react to this possible doubt, insinuated by those who indulge in the second theory, that the revelation to our saint of the mystery hidden in the womb of his spouse is postulated. In reality, one should not at all think of a doubt—even a slight one—on the part of St. Joseph, by virtue of his holiness and justice. Instead, his inner torment ought to be understood as deriving, as seems more logical, from not knowing and therefore not being able to judge fairly: this is why he prefers to withdraw and leave judgment to God. He prefers to wait for a divine intervention that will clarify what he cannot understand and therefore, above all else, he observes silence. Silence here is synonymous with prayer, with faithful expectation.

For a thorough understanding, it is beneficial to consider the most recent position on this subject, held by Fr. Tarcisio Stramare (1928–2020), a member of the Congregation of the Oblates of St. Joseph, rightly esteemed as one of the most important scholars in the field of Josephology at the international level. Starting from the post-conciliar biblical renewal, he prefers the third thesis: Joseph's withdrawal because he is overwhelmed by the greatness of the mystery. In Fr. Stramare's judgment, the traditional notion of the historicity of the Gospels understood the biblical accounts and the so-called Infancy Gospels almost as a biography of the Lord, in which the various episodes were to be coordinated and, if necessary, also integrated. Instead, the new approach, favored by *Dei Verbum* (no. 2), emphasizes not so much the description of the facts as the mystery contained in them, and therefore one should speak of the *testimony of the apostolic preaching* that goes on to form the "Gospel of the mysteries of the hidden life of Jesus." Therefore, in the story of Joseph of Nazareth, rather than seeing a chronology of events, it is necessary to scrutinize the hidden mystery that acts as the cement that binds all the stories. Why then does our saint decide to separate from his spouse? This is how Fr. Stramare replies:

> If, when confronted with his spouse who has conceived a child "by the power of the Holy Spirit" (v. 18), Joseph wishes to withdraw, it is reasonable to think, in the "context" of what we are explaining, that it was the divine "Presence" in Mary that was the true reason for his decision.[6]

Joseph's decision to distance himself from Mary because of the divine presence in her is corroborated by a new reason offered by Fr. Stramare: Mary was Joseph's first evangelizer. She was the first to communicate to him the mystery she bore in her womb:

> It is natural to think that Mary, the Annunciate Virgin, was the first to announce the Good News (which is the very meaning of the word *Gospel!*) and that the very first

---

[6] Tarcisio Stramare, *San Giuseppe: Dignità, Privilegi, Devozioni* (Camerata Picena, Italy: Shalom, 2008), 176.

person with whom she shared this is the one most beloved to her, namely, St. Joseph, who, moreover, being her true spouse, is not only the one who is the most concerned by, but also the most involved in, the mystery of her motherhood.... Let us not take away from Mary the joy and glory of having been the first evangelizer, and let us not take away from Joseph the right and privilege of being the first evangelized.[7]

This thesis according to which Mary communicates *Jesus*, the Good News, first to Joseph is certainly fascinating and probable. It seems appropriate to think that before visiting her cousin Elizabeth, to whom she brings Jesus who sanctifies John in the womb, Mary brings Jesus to Joseph, announces the Good News to him. Yet, what makes us hesitate is the fact that Joseph decides in his heart to distance himself from the mystery: from Mary and therefore from Jesus whom Mary guards in her womb as the true Ark of the Covenant.

How is it possible to reconcile Joseph's humility before the mystery with his readiness to be a minister of that mystery? Could a willingness that comes only by virtue of the angelic reassurance possibly be considered as a sign of the true humility of his heart? And why, once again, would Mary not have reassured Joseph to remain steadfast, like her, before the unveiling of the mystery? After all, he had espoused her and accepted all that might come of that union. If he had espoused a woman whom he knew to be most holy and then ascertained, thanks to his spouse, the reason for her pregnancy, so that the fulfillment of Isaiah's prophecy (7:14) would be fully revealed to him, why would he have preferred

---

[7] Ibid., 177.

to distance himself? If Joseph also necessarily had to have taken a vow of virginity, he had willingly embarked with Mary on a unique matrimonial journey, open to God's will and seeking solely to satisfy God's will. *God above all else* was Joseph's motto.

We believe that the lack of knowledge of the divine conception in Mary's womb harmonizes better with the justice of Joseph and with the humility of Mary, who, seeing herself in a completely unexpected way inhabited by the mystery, prefers to wait for God Himself to intervene and reveal His provident will to her spouse. After all, the anguish of Joseph's heart in not yet knowing the cause of conception, although nevertheless not doubting in the least the holiness of Mary, may simply be the first and most subtle co-redemptive sorrow, suffered in the secret of his heart. St. Jerome, in our opinion, indicates the clear path to follow at this juncture.

The Virginal Silence of Joseph

It is in the combination of two attributes, virginity and silence, that we can find, in my opinion, the solution to the enigma of St. Joseph at the moment when he comes to know of the pregnancy of his holy spouse. The magisteria of at least three popes have clearly taught that St. Joseph, like his spouse, also chose virginity. First, there is Pius X, who approved the litanies in honor of the saint, including the *Chaste guardian of the Virgin, Joseph most chaste,* and *Guardian of virgins*; then, there is Pius XII, who invoked St. Joseph as "virgin Guardian"; and finally, Paul VI, who speaks of "an incomparable virginal love." Moreover, Leo XIII says that Joseph is "the type and defender of virginal integrity," and before him, Pius IX had called him "*Virginum custos et pater.*" John Paul II delves into all these themes in his rich Josephine magisterium, summarized in his exhortation *Redemptoris custos*, of August 15, 1989.

A decrepit old Joseph, seen as a widower from a previous marriage, is what is presented to us by the apocryphal writings, *in primis* by the Protoevangelium of James. The concern of the apocryphal writers was to preserve the virginity of Mary and above all the divinity of Christ, preventing the spread of the error according to which Christ was Joseph's natural son. However, the iconographic tendency, starting in the fifth and sixth centuries, presents us with a young, virile, strong St. Joseph, capable of shouldering all the weight of his role as father and protector of the Holy Family. After all, Joseph of Nazareth had been given in marriage to the Ever-Virgin Mary. It would be inconceivable to imagine the man closest to Mary Most Holy as being incapable of imitating her example, precisely because Mary's virginity marked a real turning point in Christian discipleship, opening the door to Jesus' teaching on becoming eunuchs for the Kingdom of Heaven. Joseph could therefore not fail to be a mirror of Mary's virtues. In himself, he reflected Mary's love for holy virginity. Conversely, Mary had in Joseph the first devotee and disciple who had already conformed, through her example, to the highest teaching of Jesus: to leave everything and follow Him. In this, Joseph is also an icon of priestly celibacy.

The most beautiful feature that characterizes his person and that reveals his virginity is the silence of Joseph, silence before the mystery that takes place before his watchful and prayerful eyes. Joseph's silence, the attention of his heart to the will of God, is a manifestation of his highest purity of soul and body, mind, heart, and actions.

In the Angelus of December 18, 2005, Benedict XVI, commenting on John Paul II's *Redemptoris custos* on St. Joseph, described the fascinating mystery of the silence of the Saint of Nazareth:

His silence is steeped in contemplation of the mystery of God in an attitude of total availability to the divine desires. In other words, St. Joseph's silence does not express an inner emptiness but, on the contrary, the fullness of the faith he bears in his heart and which guides his every thought and action. It is a silence thanks to which Joseph, in unison with Mary, watches over the Word of God, known through the Sacred Scriptures, continuously comparing it with the events of the life of Jesus; a silence woven of constant prayer, a prayer of blessing of the Lord, of the adoration of his holy will and of unreserved entrustment to his providence. It is no exaggeration to think that it was precisely from his "father" Joseph that Jesus learned—at the human level—that steadfast interiority which is a presupposition of authentic justice, the "superior justice" which he was one day to teach his disciples.

Joseph's silence is therefore not mutism, absence of words, or lack of responsibility. It is instead Joseph's presence before the mystery, his way of standing before God. When God speaks, we must listen and let Him speak. It is the Word that speaks, the Son of God; Joseph listens to the Word and obeys. He is merely the earthly shadow of the fatherhood of God in Heaven. The supreme role of our holy carpenter is to "generate" the Son by introducing Him into the world, guiding Him during His childhood, and protecting Him with his love. Silence expresses his being a shadow, his remaining hidden and always in the background, so that Christ may be known. It is neither necessary nor prudent to depict a worn-out old Joseph to guard Mary's virginity. The nature of his role suffices to convince us of his being virile and chaste, enveloped in the strength and purity of silence. It is Christ who speaks. Joseph stands behind Him. He obeys the Word, adores Him, loves Him. Silence opens our eyes to the virginity of his heart and of his life; conversely, Joseph's virginity is the strength of his silence, a pure heart open to God, which always awaits His intervention. The pairing of virginity and silence thus brings us to the heart of another dual concept, truly central in the life of our saint: silence and justice. Joseph's silence allows us to understand well his justice, his being *for* God. He enacts justice in silence by listening *to* God. The more silence grows in him, the more justice increases, and vice versa. At the moment of conception, he does not see the Son. He listens to Him, remaining attentive to His Word. Then, when he finally sees Him, a newborn in his arms, an adolescent in his home, a man preparing for His mission, all he can do is step aside and listen. In silence.

Chapter 3

The Providential Father

In the silence of the night, while our saint enjoys some respite from the anguish he suffers in the face of the mystery as yet unveiled to his silent and prayerful heart, an angel comes to enlighten and console him. The Gospel of Matthew, after presenting to us the justice of Joseph and his suspension of all judgment when faced with the mystery, pursues thus:

> But as he considered this, behold, an angel of the Lord appeared to him in a dream, saying, "Joseph, son of David, do not be afraid to take Mary your wife, for that which is conceived in her is of the Holy Spirit; she will bear a son, and you shall call his name Jesus, for he will save his people from their sins." (Matt. 1:20–21)

The son of Mary is begotten by the Holy Spirit, but Joseph will be his father, the shadow of the heavenly Father, because he will be the one to give Him His name. In fact, only the father could give the name to the son (as we learn from Matt. 1:21), thus recognizing a legal paternity. This exceptional fatherhood of Joseph, real but at the same time supernatural, virginal, which derives exclusively from the fact that he is the spouse of the Virgin Mary, and which manifests itself in the fact that he gives the name to the Son of God, is the indispensable bond between Jesus and the house of David. Joseph is of the house and family of David, therefore of royal lineage. In fact, he went to Bethlehem, the city of David, with his spouse to be registered at the time of Jesus' birth (see Luke 2:4); to him, the angel says, "the Lord God will give to him the throne of his father David" (Luke 1:32).

Matthew, in providing us with the human genealogy of the Son of God, avoids for Joseph the verb "begot," thus abruptly interrupting the sequence of descendants, and replaces it with the legal title: "husband of Mary." Jesus is the true son of David, the true Messiah, due to the fact that He is the son of Joseph, the husband of Mary, from whom alone Jesus was born (see Matt. 1:16). For Matthew, the title of "spouse" grants Joseph that of "father," and that of "father" the Davidic genealogy of Jesus. Fr. Stramare would say that the Gospel is a fabric that does not allow for unstitching. Joseph's fatherhood is therefore real, royal, and virginal. Here, then, we have the first important fact that we can summarize with the words of John Paul II:

> Joseph's fatherhood—a relationship that places him as close as possible to Christ, to whom every election and predestination is ordered—comes to pass through marriage to Mary, that is, through the family." (*Redemptoris custos*, no. 7)

Joseph's fatherhood is recognized and exalted by the Blessed Virgin Mary when she says to Jesus, "Your father and I have been looking for you anxiously" (Luke 2:48), upon finding Him in the temple among the doctors. His fatherhood, once again, though only legal, is real, is complete: Joseph is the guardian of the Redeemer, he raises and accompanies Him in His growth, generates Him spiritually in his virginity and, by virtue of this virginal fatherhood, performs all the duties of a father toward his very own son. But more than any earthly father, Joseph is the one who watches over the mystery of the Redemption. He introduces Jesus into the world, teaches Him, as a true man, to be strong, courageous, and to always obey the will of the Father in Heaven, which Joseph knew very well and which Jesus Himself had manifested to Him upon His being found in the temple: "Did you not know that I must be in my Father's house?" (Luke 2:49).

Thus, we enter more easily into the mystery of the divine filiation of Jesus, of which Joseph of Nazareth is the guardian, having been chosen by the Father in Heaven. Joseph of Nazareth is a saint whose sublime virtues are so little known. Yet these virtues are clearly delineated in those evangelical traits of character which, thanks to a few quick brushstrokes by an expert hand, depict a figure that, in these few meager traits, manifests much, indeed the whole man. The humble carpenter of Nazareth was a modest, reserved, temperate, and silent man, along with being tenacious, as well as extraordinarily prompt and present. Joseph was present indeed, a virtue languishing so much so nowadays that men appear to be present without actually being so.

Many men are fathers but without actually being present. They bring children into the world and maintain a mere biological bond with them. They launch them into the unknown and then withdraw. They prefer to continue living in their own darkness after having dragged those poor children into the world. And so children increasingly find themselves to be fatherless and therefore no longer able to live as children. How can one then be a father if one does not know what it means to be a son? Our world, which no longer wants to be a "son" because it has rejected the Father, is increasingly experiencing the dark night of fatherlessness and the void of being a fatherless son. In some cases, we even arrive at the absurdity of two men claiming to be the fathers of the same child! Life simply becomes "a useless passion." Thus, homosexuality is becoming increasingly popular as an outlet. The fatherless look for a father elsewhere. Where are you, dear fathers? Where are you, O man? Only St. Joseph can help us out of this morass.

Joseph was a father who was always present, a true father, chosen by the eternal Father to be His reflection in time. Joseph was a man of mystery, a man of God. He had put his life in God's hands, he had placed his hands in God's hands. He let himself be led by God. He did not fear Him. He did not fear losing anything by offering himself. He offered himself and received everything: he received God Himself in his arms. For him the beatitude of the Gospel is fully realized: "Blessed are the pure in heart, for they shall see God" (Matt. 5:8). Joseph "saw" God when, in filial intimacy, he turned to the Father as to a spring where his thirst might be quenched, as to a sumptuous feast where his hunger might be satisfied. He "saw" God when he held this Son in his arms. In Jesus' humanity, Joseph saw with faith the Son of God. He lived in advance the eucharistic faith of the Church. United to his Most Holy Spouse, he believed in the divinity of Christ by contemplating His humanity. The humanity of the Son was a mirror of His divinity, just as for us who, gazing at a fragment of consecrated bread, see in it by faith all of Jesus. Joseph adored Jesus and, as father, "begot" Him with his virginal love. Joseph lived as a "son," which is why he was an extraordinary father.

Now we may ask ourselves: What exactly does the paternity of St. Joseph consist of?

His fatherhood is suffused with a supernatural mystery: he is the father of a Son begotten from eternity by the Father of Heaven and begotten in time from the Mother alone by the power of the Holy Spirit. He knows that he is called to fulfill a singular paternal mission, that of being the father of Jesus on a higher plane than the common one according to the flesh. The fatherhood of St. Joseph unfolds in the realm of the spirit. He effectively generates the Son—a generation in *agape* alone—this Son who is nevertheless the Only Begotten of the Father. Jesus has only one father, God in eternity, and one mother in time, Mary Most Holy.

The paternity of St. Joseph, therefore, is, in a singular, analogical way, a prolongation in time of the paternity of the Father of Heaven. It is the Father who calls Joseph of Nazareth to be in time the guardian of His son. He confides His son to him, placing Him in his filial hands. He chooses him to be His visible presence in the world. Therefore, Joseph begets Jesus in an analogous way—though very remote—to that of the Father in eternity. This analogy possesses both audacity and fineness. The Son proceeds from the Father always by an act of intelligence. The Father knows Himself and, knowing Himself, expresses Himself in His Word. The Son is the Father's knowledge of Himself, the mirror of His eternity. "In the beginning was the Word, and the Word was with God, and the Word was God" (John 1:1). The Word is always with the Father because it proceeds from Him. In time, the incarnate Word, who is always with the Father (see John 10:30), will remain with His earthly father in His most holy humanity. Joseph's fatherhood will then be expressed by guarding in time the eternal generation of the Son, who becomes the son of man without a father, solely with a mother.

The virginity of the love of Joseph is the treasury in which God places the mystery of Christ's divinity. Christ, who is the Son of God and of Mary, will find in Joseph, as it were, a very pure white sky that will envelop him with a spiritual whiteness, the transparency of the bosom of the Father from which He always proceeds. Joseph's pure and chaste love thus becomes a cradle for the incarnate Word, the virginal cradle of that Son who knows a paternal generation according to the Spirit alone. "God is spirit" (John 4:24) and Joseph fulfills his own role by conforming himself to God's spirituality. His affection for Jesus, his knowledge of the mystery by means of faith, will open to him the infinite mysteries of God's fatherhood, will conform him ever more to the Father. Joseph loved Jesus so much and was aware of this unique mission: *to guard in time the eternal generation of the Word*. His hands protected that Child in whom were hidden the mysteries of God. His virginal fatherhood thus becomes a *sign* of Jesus' divine filiation. In his person the invisible features of the Father will shine through. The guarantee that this Son is uniquely the Son of God, in addition to being the son of Mary's virginity, is provided by Joseph, holy man, virginal guardian of the Son, witness of the incarnate Word, image of the Father. Just as Mary's virginity will be a *sign* of Christ's divinity, so Joseph's virginity will be a *sign* of God's unique fatherhood toward this Son.

Moreover, this true fatherhood, placed on a higher plane than any earthly fatherhood, is such as to entail a relationship between Joseph as father and Jesus as son. It embraces all the mysteries of Christ's life. Fatherhood is the real relationship of the father with the child. Now, the relationship of St. Joseph with Jesus, beyond physical generation, cannot but be oriented to the whole life of Jesus and therefore to all the mysteries of His life. The life of the one who is called *pater verbi* is deeply intertwined with all the salvific mysteries of Christ. He is truly a "minister of salvation," as John Paul II put it (*Redemptoris custos*, no. 8). The father is always with the son. In all the moments of His life, he accompanies Him with his love. It is precisely the love of the father that continues to accompany the child during all the stages of His life, in dark moments as well as in happy ones: all are pedagogical moments. Joseph, therefore, cannot fail to be present in all the moments of Jesus' life. Of course, one day, before the start of the Lord's public life, he falls asleep in the arms of Jesus and Mary, but neither does he cease to remain with the Son, nor do Jesus and Mary cease to be with him, though in a new realm, that of love alone, in God, forever. All the mysteries of the Son's life therefore belong in some way also to Joseph. They involve him deeply. They allow him to participate in them. They are revealed to him in some way in advance so that he can conform himself with all his fatherly heart to these mysteries and so that, through this closeness of love, he is one with the will of the Son. Thus, the earthly father does the will of the Son, just as the Son does the will of the heavenly Father.

St. Joseph is a model father because he conformed himself perfectly to the Father. He is a model for fathers who "beget" their children according to human nature but whose generation cannot be limited to the mere biological fact. Fatherhood, St. Joseph tells us, is a mystery that must go beyond the purely physiological plane, which, moreover, is not merely accidental. He reminds us that the generation of children always and only takes place in a unique and indissoluble communion of love between a father and a mother who love one another and give themselves to one another, and who give life through the gift of self. And he also tells us that *fatherhood must go beyond this.* The father continually begets his son, even when the son has already been born. A father constantly watches over his son and "begets" him continuously in spirit. The most pernicious disorder today is, unfortunately, conceiving generation as a merely mechanical act. A child, in truth, needs to be "begotten" also in spirit. This implies paternal attention and concern for the child, education in moral values, constant care with regard to the choices he wishes to make, and a careful examination of all his requests prior to accepting or declining to meet them. As we can see, these are all spiritual activities that go beyond the initial generation, which presuppose it and perfect it, revealing the true face of fatherhood.

We need to see the father's face once again. We need God the Father who gives us His son. Let us go to Joseph: he will reveal to us the face of the truest, holiest fatherhood, the eternal one. We can summarize everything in the words of St. Augustine, which in a sculptural way give us the reason for Joseph's paternity. Why is he a father? St. Augustine responds: "He is all the more definitely and solidly the father, that he is all the more chastely the father" (*Sermo* 51, 20, 30).

The Virginal Guardian of Mary's Virginity

Joseph of Nazareth, who in a paternal manner accompanies us on our daily pilgrimage, is chosen by God the Father for a singular mission: to guard the Son of God and His Most Holy Mother. Joseph is the treasurer of the Most High and His fatherly face in time, as we have said. This paternal role leads us to consider once again his spousal role, for indeed, if Joseph is a father, it is because he is the spouse of Mary. We may thus highlight his sponsality with Mary as the interweaving of two chaste loves, as the visible manifestation of the Eternal Love. Joseph becomes the treasurer of another august mystery: Mary's virginity. He is its guardian and at the same time its witness. The virgin Mary will be delivered by the Father into his hands as into an impregnable fortress. Hence the reasonableness of St. Joseph's virginity. It is more than logical and fitting to demand that Mary's virginity be guarded by the virginity of her chaste husband and therefore to admit that St. Joseph, too, was a virgin.

Joseph of Nazareth, in reality, enters into the mystery of God through Mary, his spouse. The evangelists Matthew and Luke tell us that at the moment of the Annunciation Mary was "betrothed to a man whose name was Joseph, of the house of David" (Luke 1:27; cf. also Matt. 1:18, both using the verb *mnesteúo* = betrothed/ promised in marriage, translated by the Vulgate as *desponsata*). Only in Luke 2:5 do we read that Mary is the wife of Joseph (the same verb *mnesteúo* is used). As already noted, the Jewish marriage included an initial period of betrothal (already a true marriage), followed by cohabitation with the solemn celebration of the wedding for several days. Joseph, as Matthew tells us (1:16), is "the husband of Mary" (see also 1:19). Mary and Joseph are thus linked by a spousal love. This love opens for Joseph the immense scenarios of God's coming among us and involves both holy spouses "in the same salvific event" (John Paul II, *Redemptoris custos*, no. 1). However, a difficulty apparently arises. How is it that Mary, presented to us by Luke (1:27) as "the virgin" and as Joseph's "betrothed," is able to make a promise, a vow of virginity in her heart? This is clearly evident in her words: "How can this be, for I have no husband?" (Luke 1:34), in reply to the angel who asked her to become the Mother of God. Luke faithfully conveys to us two mysteries: the Incarnation of the Son of God by the Virgin Mary by the power of the Holy Spirit, and the fact that this mystery took place within the framework of the institution of marriage. Without denying either mystery, it is instead a question of considering marriage on a higher level, so as to foresee the possibility of a vow of virginity not only for Mary but also for Joseph.

How, then, can Mary's vow be reconciled with the fact that she must cohabit with Joseph? St. Thomas Aquinas, in asking this question, starts from the observation that it was fitting that Mary's virginity was consecrated to God by a vow (*Summa Theologica*, III, q. 28, art. 4). Certainly, Our Lady had the desire to remain a virgin even before her marriage to Joseph. However, if she had vowed to do so before marriage, such a vow would have rendered the marital consent invalid, unless it had been made by common consent of the spouses. St. Thomas offers a very insightful solution. Mary, he says, took a vow of virginity before marriage "in desire" and in a conditional form, saying, for example, "if it pleases God," or "if God wills it" (see St. Thomas's *Commentary on Matthew's Gospel*).

This is also because her vow was not something made lightly, as the book of Numbers (30:8–9) reminds us. For if her husband had known of such a vow and had opposed it, he would have annulled it, and with it, the obligation taken on lightly. It was an obligation pondered in her heart and thus, with deep desire, brought to the heart of her chaste husband as well. Once married, says Aquinas, "When she had understood that this was acceptable to God, 'together with' Joseph, and before the angelic announcement, Mary took the vow of virginity in an absolute manner" (*Summa Theologica*, III, q. 28, art. 4). Mary therefore took a vow of absolute chastity after her marriage and before the angel's announcement.

It is also fitting to think, again with Aquinas, that the Blessed Virgin had been reassured by God, before contracting marriage with Joseph, that he also cultivated in his heart the same holy desire and therefore did not expose himself to danger by marrying, his virginity remaining unharmed (*Super Sententiarum*, bk. 4, d. 30, q. 2, a. 1, qc. 2, ad 2; *Summa Theologica*, III, q. 29, art. 1, ad 1). With Fr. Tarcisio Stramare, then, it must be concluded that Mary's word to the angel, "I know not man," "does not deny, in fact, the reality of conjugal union, but reveals a purpose of virginity, the possibility of which in that context can only be explained by supposing the certainty of having already received the relative 'gift of self' from the bridegroom." Hence his very important theological conclusion: "Because of the intimate and universal sense of the faithful, it can be affirmed that Joseph's virginity is theologically very certain and closely tied to the faith"[8]

There is also a notable patristic motif that highlights the providential character of the marriage between the two holy spouses, which aims to conceal the virginal conception of Jesus from the devil. Joseph thus acts as the guardian of Mary's virginity, of Jesus' divine nature and therefore of the salvific value of the mystery of the Cross, against the devil and his machinations. In fact, the devil often tried to find out from Jesus whether He was truly the Son of God (in particular at the moment of the temptations in the desert, Matt. 4:1–11) in order to hinder His journey toward the Cross and therefore the mystery of the expiatory Redemption of the human race. Joseph is the guardian of all these divine mysteries, concealing *first of all* the virginity of his spouse. This is a very profound thought that is expressed by St. Ignatius of Antioch († 107/110) before being taken up and given a deeper Josephine note by Origen, St. Basil, St. Ambrose, St. Jerome, and others. Here, for example, is what Origen says in his commentary on the Gospel of Luke, highlighting the role of Joseph:

> The virginity of Mary remained hidden from the prince of this century. She remained hidden because of Joseph; she remained hidden because of marriage; she remained hidden because she was considered married. For if she had

---

[8] Stramare, *San Giuseppe*, 188–189.

not had a bridegroom, and, as was believed, a husband, in no way could she have remained hidden from the prince of this world. For immediately the tacit thought of the devil would have crept in: how could she, who was not joined to a man, have become pregnant? This conception must be divine, it must be something more sublime than human nature. (*Homily 6*)

In the words of St. Augustine, St. Joseph is "the witness to the virginity of the bride" (*Sermo* 51, 6, 9). The espousal with Mary then introduces St. Joseph into the mystery of salvation and makes him an active participant in every event concerning Jesus, his son. By welcoming Mary as his wife, St. Joseph sees himself involved in the mystery of the Redemption. By saying his virginal *yes* to Mary, he prepares himself to say his yes to the Redemption. Joseph is the man who said yes to God because he welcomed Mary into his life. The Virgin, his wife, introduces him into the mystery of God, into the mystery of the Son of God. He willingly accepts it. He is ready to do God's will. He was a man who put God, the Truth, first. Everything was in view of God, and he himself, through Mary, put himself at the service of universal salvation.

The yes to Mary is always a yes to God. Joseph's yes to his bride and Mary's yes to Joseph are an interweaving and a bond of pure love that unites them in Christ and for Christ. Joseph loves the Virgin Mary and Mary loves the chaste Joseph in such a profound and perfect way that this love will prepare the Incarnation and accompany Jesus in His mysteries. This virginal love of His parents will be the human strength of the Son in always doing the will of the Father. How important is the love of parents for their children!

Given those traits that, though few, depict Joseph as being so full of holiness, we can easily dismiss the sheer gratuitousness of imagining that he might have had the least shadow of a doubt about Mary's integrity. After the initial start of surprise, filling him with a holy perplexity in the face of the mystery of the conception of his bride, he did not hesitate to trust in his God, and from Him he received light. Informed of the divine intervention, he immediately "took his wife" with him (Matt. 1:24).

In that verb "took" (*parélaben* in Greek, *accepit* in Latin), we can perceive his yes to God through Mary; his yes to the Child Jesus, and therefore to the mystery of the Redemption, already contained in the name that he would impose on his son (see Matt. 1:21: in this the Hebrew Matthew sums up Joseph's legal paternity of Jesus, who was born only of Mary, see 1:16). Joseph "took" Mary, he welcomed her, more than merely *with* him, but rather, *in* himself, in his life, in his most intimate fibers, in his heart.

This is the same verb used by John (albeit in the simple form of *élaben*) to describe the testament of Jesus dying on the Cross who gives the disciple to Mary, His mother, and the Mother to the disciple. The beloved disciple, from that moment, took Mary into his home (John 19:27). He took Mary, more precisely, among his belongings, among his most intimate things.

Our Lady has been given to the beloved disciple to be his spiritual mother. Indeed, John welcomes Mary, the Woman, who has now become his mother. The mother of Jesus is the mother of John, precisely insofar as she is the Woman, that is, the New Eve beside the New Adam. This is a thought very dear to the Apostolic Fathers. Mary, the Woman, is associated with Christ: she is the Co-redemptrix. The term *woman* certainly recalls the name given by Adam to her, who was extracted from him so that she could be a help that would correspond to him (see Gen. 2:23), so that she might be one with him.

The role of John and of Mary on Calvary is a representative role. John represents every disciple of Christ and Mary the mother of every child of God, born in the pangs of that salvific co-redemption, united with the Redemption of Christ. Jesus' commands "Woman, behold thy son" and "Behold thy mother" echo His command imparted at the Last Supper to repeat the sacrificial-sacramental gesture in memory of Him (see Luke 22:19). Precisely in the light of the "hour" of Calvary, the "hour" of our salvation, in which Mary's acceptance is fundamental in order for us to be fully introduced into the salvific mystery of Christ, we can grasp the salvific significance of that first welcome that Joseph made of his spouse.

Many years before Jesus gave Mary to John, Joseph took Mary, the "Woman" present at the "hour" of her Son. In her and through her he became a participant in the mystery of Christ which culminated in the bloody Redemption of Calvary. His marriage with the Blessed Virgin was lived in the light of that "hour," which was now imbued with ineffable joys: that of guarding the mystery of the God made flesh in his hands and in his life, and of guarding the tabernacle of God, his spouse. It was an hour of sorrow and suffering: the flight into Egypt, the interior drama of knowing his son was being sought after in order to be slain, the paternal sorrow caused by the sword that would pierce Mary's heart according to the words of Simeon in the presentation of the Child Jesus in the temple (Luke 2:33–35), a sword that, in return, would strike his own heart with a flaming dart of love and sorrow. Although "his father and his mother marveled at what was said about him" (Luke 2:33), those other impressive words—"This child is set for the fall and rising of many" (Luke 2:34)—pierced

Mary's heart as with a stake, while simultaneously piercing the heart of her chaste spouse. Joseph and Mary were united by one love, the love of Jesus the Savior.

The marriage with Mary was immediately seen as a salvific co-participation in the mystery of the Redemption. Thus, Joseph's spousal fidelity was fidelity above all to God who had become an infant, with the desire to love Him above all things, to serve Him, to make His love shine through his own love. Only when love is rooted in eternal Love does it become true, stable, imperishable.

Mary was for Joseph a reflection of the light of God, the love that flowed from the triune and eternal Love. Moreover, Mary was Joseph's way to God. She was the Mediatrix between God her son and Joseph, the virginal father of Jesus: father of Jesus because spouse of Mary. His sponsality with Mary opened to him the infinite horizons of divine life, of the completion of Christ's sufferings for the sake of the ecclesial body (cf. Col. 1:24). Joseph was able to participate actively in the mystery of the Redemption by means of Mary, in his sponsality with Mary. He is the model of the co-redemptive co-participation of every child of God who is reborn in Mary's womb, in the nuptials of love with the Virgin Mother.

Mary is the unique way to Christ. Through Mary, one is actively grafted into the salvation of Christ. Through Mary, we are bound to Jesus. Joseph of Nazareth, Mary's spouse, is her most authoritative witness and, at the same time, the exemplary prototype of men redeemed in the blood of Jesus and in the tears of Mary.

Now that we have sketched out the portrait of Joseph, the just and righteous man who, through Mary, as her spouse, becomes the father and guardian of the Word made flesh, and enters into the mystery of salvation, which he safeguards and which he wholeheartedly espouses, we are able to delve more deeply into his role in the mystery of salvation. Before doing so, however, let us take a moment to consider, alongside the Heart of Joseph, another holy place that serves as a sign and a safeguard for the divine mystery of the Incarnation.

Chapter 4

The Cave of Bethlehem, Figure of the Heart of Joseph

The Heart of holy Joseph is the place of his virginal purity, his humble silence, his prompt obedience, and his steadfast fidelity to God. It is the interior fortress that allows him to serve as the safeguard of the sacred mysteries of his holy Spouse's virginity and of the Son's divinity.

As we have seen, if one were to suppose a doubt on the part of Joseph regarding Mary's integrity, this would entail a diminishing of the mystery. If one were to imagine any siblings for Jesus, by misinterpreting Scripture, this would likewise dim the mystery, to the point of dissolving the divine in a purely worldly vision. In a similar way, to the humble and silent Joseph, the cave of Bethlehem also serves to safeguard the holy mystery, veiled as it is in the silence of the night and the humility of the place. The modest and discreet cave is thus a figure of the meek and silent Heart of Joseph, both of which signify by their very simplicity and discretion a separation from all that is profane and a consecration to the divine.

Just as the Heart of Joseph, full of virginal purity, is the place where the divine mystery of the Incarnation is conceived, through the mediation of Mary, his spouse, enabling him to be God's providence here below, safeguarding the Mother and the Child, so likewise the cave—pure virgin earth where God's infinity enters its infancy—is the place where the God-Man first manifests Himself to the world. Both are the humble home of the mystery as it unfolds in time and both must be maintained in the hearts of the faithful as signs of the virginal purity of the Faith and of the transcendent beauty of the divine mystery, in all its glorious humility.

The Birthplace of Jesus, Sign of the Mystery

Let us allow ourselves a moment of digression to reflect, in the company of St. Joseph, on the importance of the birthplace of Jesus, identified by a solid and ancient tradition, as having taken place in a poor cave in Bethlehem. Recent studies have attempted to locate the birth of Jesus in a commonplace dwelling of the time, not realizing, however, that in this way, not only is there a risk of denying the mystery of the incarnate Word, and of disregarding the virginity of Mary but also of rendering irrelevant and meaningless the relationship between sign and reality which is so central in the Gospels in order to lead to the faith firstly the shepherds, then the Magi, and finally all of us. It is precisely Joseph of Nazareth, a silent witness of the mystery that took place on that holy night, who instructs us on the intimate relationship between the "sign" and the Child. It is he who, with Mary, "shows" to the shepherds her son, the Son of God (see Luke 2:16). It is he who helps us to understand the mystery of Jesus' birth in order to preserve the whole mystery of Christ and the intact virginity of his spouse. Let us examine the problem.

The Testimonies of Tradition

In the Gospels we have little historical data about Jesus' birth. What we do have, however, is sufficient to preserve the mystery. From St. Matthew and St. Luke, we learn that Jesus was born in Bethlehem of Judea (Matt. 2:1; Luke 2:4). From St. Luke we learn only that there was no room "at the inn" (or "at the lodging") and that, for this reason, the Child was wrapped in swaddling clothes and laid in a manger (Luke 2:4–7; *phátne*). The traditional view holds that Jesus was born in a cave.

The Scriptures do not mention a cave, of course. However, there are historical witnesses among the early Church Fathers who attest to Jesus' being born in a cave: St. Justin Martyr (A.D. 150), according to whom Jesus was born in a cave that was used as a stable, though not the typical stone and wooden stable so commonplace in our Christian art. Then there is Origen (A.D. 250), followed by St. Jerome (A.D. 325). In A.D. 335, Emperor Constantine built the Basilica of the Nativity on the spot where the cave of Jesus' Nativity had been identified in Bethlehem, thanks to the historical testimonies of these early Church Fathers.

Let's now consider the following hypothesis: If the very grotto of Jesus' birth in Bethlehem, upon which the Basilica of the Nativity was built, should no longer be considered the birthplace of Our Lord in light of a new exegetical interpretation, could this new position simply call into question the now centuries-old belief in the historical authenticity of such an ancient site? Indeed, the site of the grotto had ironically been preserved by the emperor Hadrian in his attempt to desecrate the Jewish and Christian holy places in Palestine shortly after 130. The crux of the matter, upon which the whole affair would appear to be hanging, is a different translation of one single word. Is this sufficient ground for dismissing the traditional belief?

Was There No Room in the Guest Room?

Why does this question hinge upon a single word? In recent decades, starting especially with the studies of Kenneth Bailey (1930–2016, Presbyterian minister, prolific author, and lecturer in Middle Eastern New Testament studies), in particular his work titled *Jesus through Middle Eastern Eyes: Cultural Studies in the Gospels* (2008), this classical view has been called into question and a new theory has been favored: Jesus would have been born in an ordinary house. Bailey follows the interpretation of Alfred Plummer (1841–1926, Church of England clergyman and biblical scholar) in his *Gospel According to St. Luke* (5th ed., International Critical Commentary, 1922).

There are several arguments supporting this theory. First, there is the fact that it would have been nearly impossible for Joseph, being of the house of David and finding himself in Bethlehem, a royal city, not to find a place where Mary, his wife, could give birth. It would have been unthinkable to imagine him knocking at any door, reciting his royal genealogy, and not being welcomed for the night. This apparent incongruity leads to a second and more important exegetical argument. The word used by Luke to indicate the inn, in which there was no room for the Holy Family, is *katáluma* (from *katá lúo)*, meaning to unloose or untie, that is, to unsaddle one's horses and untie one's pack, which can mean a lodging place for men and cattle. In fact, there are authors, such as Joseph Fitzmyer S.J., in *The Gospel according to Luke I–IX* (1970), who translate *katáluma* with "lodge," a sort of caravansary. For Raymond E. Brown, in *The Birth of the Messiah* (1977), Luke seems more interested in telling his audience where Mary laid the newborn baby. The fact that the details about the swaddling clothes and the manger are repeated three times (Luke 2:7, 12, 16) must be of considerable significance, setting this unique scene against the lack of space at the various lodgings. The mention of the lodgings is of minor importance. It is not the focus, although for Brown, who conducts his research according to a pure historical-critical method, "If the manger was pre-Lucan in the tradition, the lack of place in the lodgings may have been Luke's vague surmise, in order to explain the use of the manger."[9]

What if it was instead the historical account of what truly happened? Why exclude this *a priori*? There is a very manifest attempt to explain the birth of Our Lord with its various suggestive details as a *Midrash* (interpretating or commenting on a word or an event in the Old Testament as reproduced in the New, by considering it to be a theological interpretation of the evangelist, with no historical foundation). And yet, one should recall that the birth of Our Lord, as related in the Gospels, is unique in its own genre. What Scott Hahn says of Matthew's Gospel can also be applied to Luke's:

> Unlike midrash, the evangelist's story of Jesus is not founded on an Old Testament text. Whereas midrash seeks to mine deeper meanings of the Old Testament, Matthew does not seek to interpret the Old Testament for its own sake. More to the point, Matthew is not retelling Old Testament episodes but is telling an entirely new story! It is a story with new characters and events; it is a story that could stand on its own apart from his Old Testament citations. Matthew employs the Old Testament

---

[9] Raymond E. Brown, *The Birth of the Messiah: A Commentary on the Infancy Narratives in Matthew and Luke* (London: Chapman, 1977; repr. 1978), 419.

to illuminate the significance of Jesus' birth, not to determine in advance its plot and outcome.[10]

It is true, however, that when Luke does mention a proper "inn," in the parable of the Good Samaritan who takes care of the man who had fallen among thieves (Luke 10:34), he uses the more general term *pandocheîon*, meaning a commercial inn, where travelers and guests were typically welcomed. *Katáluma*, more specifically, is the word for the private "upper" room where Jesus celebrates the Last Supper with His disciples (Mark 14:14 and Luke 22:11; Matthew does not mention the room). This is clearly a reception or guest room in a private home. The reading of *katáluma* as a "guest room" is here preferred for the fact that in the Gospel of Luke two elements already encountered would be in opposition with one another: *phátne* and *katáluma*, designating the latter as a space in various types of structures. Hence, the conclusion is that it is likely that Mary and Joseph were hosted in the only room intended for the family, which served as a living room and bedroom, where there was also enough room for the animals, with a feeding trough, either carved in the floor or built as a freestanding element, since there was no available guest room. Mary would therefore have given birth to Jesus in the middle of a crowded house, in the presence of guests and relatives, even if only women, who also acted as midwives, were admitted at the moment of childbirth. The shepherds would arrive and find such a festive atmosphere that they could announce the good news to all the people there gathered. Bailey concludes his analyses thus:

[10] Scott Hahn, *Ignatius Catholic Study Bible: The New Testament* (San Francisco: Ignatius Press, 2010) 10.

Our Christmas crèche sets remain as they are because "ox and ass before him bow, / for he is in the manger now." But that manger was in a warm and friendly home, not in a cold and lonely stable. Looking at the story in this light strips away layers of interpretative mythology that have built up around it. Jesus was born in a simple two-room village home such as the Middle East has known for at least three thousand years. Yes, we must rewrite our Christmas plays, but in rewriting them, the story is enriched, not cheapened.[11]

The Dimming of Some Tenets of Faith

In truth, by following this apparently convincing theory, aiming above all at comforting Jesus and the Holy Spouses by delivering them from such a cold scenario of isolation as depicted by Tradition, one risks calling into question some basic truths of the Faith, albeit in a veiled way. This should be of import to all Christians and not just Catholics. First, let us ask ourselves: What would constitute the "sign" of the miraculous birth of the Messiah, true God and true man, if the environment was that of a normal family home, where the joyful and festive atmosphere would have been caused by the gathering of relatives and acquaintances who had come to Bethlehem for the census rather than for the birth of the Messiah? Would Jesus have been the protagonist of Christmas in that crowded house? The "sign" of His birth expresses the miracle and must be at once transcendent and comprehensible, both to the simple and to the learned, to everyone. Similarly, what "sign"

---

[11] Kenneth Bailey, *Jesus through Middle Eastern Eyes: Cultural Studies in the Gospels* (Downers Grove, IL: IVP Academic, 2008), 36.

of the divinity of Christ would remain were one to deny the virginal integrity of Mary and Joseph?

The sign was a "babe wrapped in swaddling cloths and lying in a manger" (Luke 2:12). If Jesus had been laid in a manger inside a house, this would rather have represented a normal place where animals were fed, and would not have pointed to anything special, beyond its immediate, tangible, meaning. If the inhabitants of Bethlehem were so hospitable, why not offer that Child a more comfortable place, a simple cushion, or something similar on which to lay Him, rather than a hollow in the floor? But what clashes most with the Gospel account is the fact that when the shepherds arrived, they did not find a crowd but simply those who are, with the Child, the protagonists of the mystery of Christmas. "They went with haste," the Gospel notes, "and found Mary and Joseph, and the babe lying in a manger" (Luke 2:16). They found only three people, who were certainly enveloped in a silence expressive of adoration. In fact, silence and solitude foster the presence of the mystery. Luke presents Joseph as being closest to Jesus. With this brief remark, the evangelist wishes to manifest his true fatherhood: a relationship which, in the words of John Paul II, places our saint "as close as possible to Christ" (*Redemptoris custos*, no. 7). Why may we not then think that it was Joseph himself in this context, together with his spouse, the two of them alone, who opened the hearts of the shepherds to the mystery hidden in that Infant? With his fatherly delicacy he gazed at Him, adored Him, begged Him, and thus also inflamed the hearts of those zealous pilgrims who had just arrived.

Moreover, if the shepherds had arrived at a private home in the city of Bethlehem, would they have been welcomed, since their social status, due to their *unclean* profession, excluded them from civic life? Unless we are tempted to deny the historicity of the shepherds coming to the manger, we should also remember that these humble and rejected people were inscribed on a list of those ineligible to be judges or witnesses since they grazed their flocks on other people's land. Besides being held as unclean, they were also labeled as dishonest. How, then, might we reconcile their social exclusion on the one hand with the likelihood of their being welcomed in a private home on the other? Moreover, their evangelizing zeal, telling everyone about the baby, leaving the people who heard their message in a state of wonder (see Luke 2:17–18), begins only after the encounter with Christ and by the effective means of His grace. They arrived, the Gospel recounts, *saw* the sign as foretold them by the angel, and *understood* the word spoken to them concerning the Child (see Luke 2:17).

Would they have seen and understood if that room had been occupied by strangers to the miraculous event? What would have been so special about the encounter, moreover, if all the people to whom the shepherds announced the great tidings had been in the house where Mary and Joseph were? Would there have been a need to evangelize those relatives and guests, if they were already aware of the presence of the Holy Family?

The focus is on the *sign* of the *manger*, thanks to which the birthplace also shares in being a sign of the uniqueness of that Child, the newborn Messiah. The singularity of that birth had to be grasped by extraordinary exterior elements, leading to an interior reality, easily understandable. Seeing the sign and acknowledging the truthfulness of the angel's word, they came straight to the following conclusion: this Child is Christ the Savior. We may well suppose that the shepherds were the first to be called, for the fact that they, in some way, experienced the same condition as the newborn Messiah, that of the *anawim*, to which Mary and Joseph belonged. But they were also the only people to remain awake at night, keeping watch over their flocks. They were vigilant in the night of that world, and ready, in their humility, for God's coming. With simplicity and trust, they welcomed the word of the angel and set out on their journey of faith toward the newborn Savior. The Gospel says: "And when they saw it they made known the saying which had been told them concerning this child" (Luke 2:17). The word spoken to them meant the *sign*, and the sign now points back to the word and reassures them, allows them to believe. Word and sign are one in the flesh assumed by the Logos and express the sacramental unity of the invisible and visible reality in the sacrament *par excellence*: the Word incarnate.

However, there is another important fact to reflect on, and which is decisive: If Our Lady had given birth in a normal house, with people coming and going and with women assisting her, the logical conclusion would have been that the childbirth was not virginal. An ordinary familial context evokes immediately an ordinary childbirth. An external condition appropriate to the virginal childbirth was needed so that it might be wrapped up by silence, *privacy*, and the intimacy between the Mother and the Son. Even Joseph's presence is not required in that solemn moment. The virginity *in partu* of the Mother is a miraculous, extraordinary birth of the Son, of the One who comes through the womb of the Blessed Virgin without touching it, with neither rupture nor birth pangs. That moment preludes Jesus' Resurrection, when His glorious body came through the linen cloths, leaving them lying as they had enveloped His body, which was truly astonishing for John and Peter. John *saw* this sign and *believed* in the Resurrection (see John 20:4–8); it also preludes Our Lord's entering the upper room, again after His Resurrection, passing through a closed door (see John 20:19). The way Jesus came into the world is reflected in these solemn later moments of His life, interwoven with the experience of silence and seclusion from profane eyes. The mystery is sacred, necessarily set apart from profanity, otherwise it is easily denied. The birth in a normal home environment, in spite of a traditional and constant belief, conveys the idea of a "normal" moment in the life of Joseph and Mary, where, in fact, the mystery is obscured by the noise and profanity of life. Furthermore, the theory of a "living room" as Jesus' birthplace seems to favor the idea of a joyful Christmas, where no isolation and sadness were experienced by the Infant Jesus, immersed rather in a festal atmosphere. And yet it seems to spoil, in addition to the very tenets of the Faith, the true meaning of joy, and therefore of celebration.

Joy is brought about by the Nativity of Christ, by the *fact* of His birth and not by the external situation of a warm familial environment. It is the virginal childbirth of Mary, painless, joyful, and peaceful, that announces an unparalleled joy to be transmitted to the world. The shepherds were the first to become messengers of this joy because they experienced it themselves: a joy beyond human expectation. Now, all those who heard the humble shepherds speak of the Child wondered at the good tidings they were spreading all around: Christ the Lord was born. And Mary, the Mother of Jesus, the one who was fully aware of the virginal mystery of the Incarnation and Birth of Emmanuel, "kept all these things, pondering them in her heart" (Luke 2:19). Mary keeps the words of the shepherds, their faith in the mystery of God's Incarnation as echoing the word of the celestial messenger. Her Immaculate Heart guarded the first fruits of that faith: it is the holy place where all the mysteries of faith, as well as the wonder and awe of the first believers, are kept secure. One last argument to refute the hypothesis of a living room as

Jesus' birthplace is offered precisely in this: Mary's interior and highly spiritual attitude in meditating on those words. From this is conveyed once again the idea of an atmosphere of recollection, silence, and solitude that enveloped the birth of that Child. Only Mary was with the Child at the wonderful moment of His coming into this world, and therefore the Child was with Mary. Mother and Son, Son and Mother, are one and remain in that virginal oneness.

The Child with Mary His Mother

To be convinced of this virginal unity between the Child and His mother, necessarily to be echoed by a suitable exterior environment, one can also make reference to St. Matthew's Gospel. Here, the virginity of Mary serves as a golden thread uniting in a special manner the Son with the Mother. Matthew, in chapter 2, repeats five times the same expression, namely that the *Child Jesus is with Mary His mother*. Let us analyze these expressions that very significantly seem to reiterate a "liturgical formula." The context is the visit of the Magi and the flight into Egypt, followed by the return of the Holy Family to Nazareth.

> 2:11: And going into the house they saw the *child with Mary his mother*, and they fell down and worshiped him.

> 2:13: Now when they had departed, behold, an angel of the Lord appeared to Joseph in a dream and said: "Rise, take *the child and his mother*, and flee to Egypt."

> 2:14: And he rose and took *the child and his mother* by night, and departed to Egypt.

> 2:20: Rise, take *the child and his mother*, and go to the land of Israel.

2:21: And he rose and took *the child and his mother*, and went to the land of Israel.

It is clear that the Child is indissolubly united with Mary, His mother, and that the bond of unity between them is the perpetual virginity of Mary. Jesus is the only son of Mary, without a father, as He is the only son of the Father in Heaven, without a mother, true God and true man. We can summarize it all with the famous motto by St. Louis-Marie Grignion de Montfort: *ad Jesum per Mariam*.

In the silence of Mary's virginity, in her divine discretion, we find the true cradle of the holy birth of Jesus, which necessarily reflects and shapes the material one: the austere cave of the birth of the Divine Child. Yet even now, St. Joseph is the guardian of the mystery: of the virginity of Mary and of the divinity of Jesus.

In the middle of that night, he provided for a makeshift accommodation in a poor cave. Even those poor and bare walls became the medium of a great mystery. Either the mystery is a unity of sign and reality, or it simply vanishes into thin air. Just as the humble Heart of holy Joseph was like virgin earth, always ready to accommodate the mystery of the Child through the mediation of his holy Spouse, so likewise this simple cave is made ready by his diligent hands to be a holy though humble place in order to welcome the sacred mystery, far from all profanity, in the solemn silence of the holy night.

Part 2

Co-Redeemer with Christ and Guardian of the Church

By way of introduction to our theological reflections on the place of Joseph in the eternal designs of God the Father, let us contemplate this unusual enamel plaque, which illustrates a deep mystery in the life of our discreet saint. Joseph is depicted holding the knife that he will employ in order to circumcise the Child Jesus, held tenderly in the arms of His mother. The uniqueness of this depiction consists precisely in this fact that it is Joseph who is shown as accomplishing the rite of circumcision, rather than a priest of the Old Covenant, as is customary in most religious artworks. Let us now envisage the scene through the eyes of St. Joseph:

With holy fear filling his heart and the virtue of religion ruling his will, he approaches the Child and His mother, whose mutual embrace he lovingly admires. Placing the cloth which he carries on her lap as on an altar—the true altar of the temple in which the Holy Family is enshrined—he prepares himself through prayer, while Mary gently places the Child on the linen. As he obediently fulfills his role as a father, whose duty it is to make the cut in the flesh of the Son, he sees the very first drop of that Precious Blood which, he knows, is being shed for the salvation of mankind. He contemplates this single drop of blood and perceives, as it were, the whole wide world enclosed therein, all awash in crimson. This tiny droplet alone suffices to cleanse mankind of sin. Next, with head bowed low, he adores the sacred mystery unfolding before his eyes, and then, raising his eyes heavenward, he offers to the Father this first drop of blood shed by the Savior, simultaneously sacrificing himself along with his son. With his most pure Heart, inwardly bleeding throughout this sacrificial rite, he knowingly and willingly exercises his priestly mediation, not as an ordained priest, offering the sacrifice sacramentally, but partaking in this initial foreshadowing of the unique bloody sacrifice to come, through a spiritual priesthood of a higher order. Fully imbued with the sacerdotal spirit of the High Priest, his son, Joseph knows that

> Unlike anyone else, Our Lord came on earth, not to live, but to die. Death for our redemption was the goal of His sojourn here, the gold that He was seeking ... He was, therefore, not primarily a teacher, but a Saviour ... Was not Christ the Priest a Victim? ... He never offered anything except Himself ... So, we have a mutilated concept of our priesthood, if we envisage it apart from making ourselves victims in the prolongation of His Incarnation.[12]

The humble and pure Heart of Holy Joseph is fully imbued with the spirit of victimhood inherent to the priestly vocation. Through his limitless self-offering, he is indeed the exemplar of priestly fatherhood, of each and every priest, who must seek to become as pure and holy as Joseph. No one would deny that Holy Mother Church, in the person of her ministers, is currently suffering from a crisis of spiritual fatherhood, mirroring that of

---

[12] Fulton Sheen, *The Priest Is Not His Own* (New York: McGraw Hill, 1963), 1–2.

natural fatherhood in society at large, though more gravely due to the higher nature of this supernatural paternity. The remedy resides in a renewed sense of self-offering on the part of the priest who, as *alter Christus*, must be a holy victim, like the Christ Child and Holy Joseph in this mystery we now consider. Meditating on this sacrificial offering of St. Joseph can help lead to a renewal of the sacrificial nature of priestly fatherhood, by inciting the priest to embrace the victimhood of Jesus and the co-victimhood of Joseph. To heal the woundedness of the Mystical Body caused by this crisis of spiritual fatherhood, Heaven has provided a flawless solution: "Ite ad Ioseph," "Go to Joseph."

Chapter 5

A Preeminent Sanctity in View of a Preeminent Mission

The portrait we have sketched of Joseph as righteous man, virginal spouse and providential father, guardian of the mystery of the virginity of Mary and of the divinity of Jesus, spurs us to consider more precisely the nature of the unique mission entrusted to him by the Father. And the grandeur of St. Joseph's role in the accomplishing of the mystery of salvation will incite us then to discern how the Father, in His eternal foresight, provided the graces and privileges in adequation with the fulfilling of this mission. Thus, we will now address a central topic in Josephine theology: the unique and unparalleled nature of St. Joseph's mission from which its singularity shines forth. Conversely, we can also say that its singularity derives from the unique mission that the holy Carpenter of Nazareth received from God.

The moment has therefore come to reflect more deeply on the mission of St. Joseph in order to see its implications with regard to his fullness of grace, his participation in the order of the hypostatic union, by virtue of a special grace conferred on him, and his eternal predestination.

Joseph's unique mission thus reveals to us his equally unique holiness, beyond all the patriarchs, prophets, apostles, and even

John the Baptist himself. His holiness is far superior to that of the greatest martyrs and the most eminent Doctors of the Church. This may at first appear to be an excess of zeal and devotion toward a humble carpenter of whom hardly a word is spoken, and yet this is the most attested doctrine that, from the sixteenth century onwards, has become increasingly commonplace, having been upheld by great saints and eminent theologians. Suffice it to mention St. Teresa, St. Francis de Sales, St. Bernardine of Siena, St. Alphonsus de Liguori, Gerson, Suárez, Fr. Isidoro de Isolanis, Cardinal Alexis-Henri-Marie Lépicier, Fr. Réginald Garrigou-Lagrange, and so on.

According to the commonly held theological principle, it is very fitting that, here on earth, the fullness of grace created in the soul of the Savior, along with the holiness of the Virgin Mary, and even the faith of the apostles, should be in conformity with the specific divine mission entrusted to them. The mission is proportionate to the holiness or, one could even say: a special mission requires an equally special degree of grace in order that the former may be accomplished. The closer one is to Christ, the source of holiness, the more one is enriched with that grace that enables one to be like Him by bringing one's mission to its fulfillment. The same can likewise be said of St. Joseph who, after his spouse, is closest to Jesus, and therefore is, after her, the most enriched of all saints. Yet, Jesus' words relating to John the Baptist seem instead to contradict this principle by designating the Precursor as the "greatest." Jesus says that "Among those born of women there has risen no one greater than John the Baptist; yet he who is least in the kingdom of heaven is greater than he" (Matt. 11:11). John is certainly the greatest of his predecessors in the Old Testament. In fact, this is how St. Thomas Aquinas, in his commentary on this pericope, expounds the greatness of John the Baptist. He is greater and more excellent by virtue of the office entrusted to him: to prepare the way for the Lord. Abraham was the greatest of the patriarchs for his faith and Moses for the office of prophecy. In fact, even of the latter we read (in Deut. 34:10) that "There has not arisen a prophet since in Israel like Moses." All of them were precursors of the Lord and John is the Precursor *par excellence* as he is closer to Jesus and the last in comparison with all the saints of the Old Testament. That is why in the litanies of the saints, as Aquinas also points out, he is placed immediately after the Blessed Virgin Mary and the angels. The Old Testament ends, and the New Testament begins, with John the Baptist.

However, Our Lord also adds that "He who is least in the kingdom of heaven is greater than he" (Matt. 11:11). Now, comments Garrigou-Lagrange, if the kingdom of God here on earth is the Church now present, who in the Church is the smallest and the least? It is he who has the greatest degree of charity while making himself the servant of all, even though he is the greatest (see Luke 22:26). He who is designated as the least, and so, who is greater than John the Baptist, is neither an apostle, nor an evangelist, nor a pontiff, nor a Doctor, nor a priest—but he who, no less than the apostles and evangelists and Doctors, knew and loved Christ. He is none other than the humble Carpenter of Nazareth, Joseph.[13]

The smallest, the least of all, is ultimately Jesus Himself. Next are those who, like Him, have become small: Mary and then Joseph, as they were mutually bound, in a hierarchical manner, to

---

[13] Chap. 7, "St. Joseph's Pre-eminence over All Other Saints," in Réginald Garrigou-Lagrange, *Mother of the Saviour and Our Interior Life* (Saint Louis, MO: Herder, 1949).

the unique grace that came from the incarnate Word, allowing them to participate in His fullness of grace and in the order of the hypostatic union of the divine Word with humanity. All other saints come only after this order of grace and greatness.

The Gift of the Fullness of Grace

Our dear St. Joseph received from God many gifts, all of them truly extraordinary by virtue of his unique mission. The first to venture, through theological reflection, into the vast mystery of his exceptional participation in the fullness of the grace of Christ was the Dominican Father Isidoro Isolani (ca. 1480–1528), author of the first great work of a theological and devotional nature dedicated to St. Joseph, titled *Summa de donis S. Ioseph* (1522). Fr. Isolani defines the fullness of grace, from whose abundance all gifts of grace emanate, as being twofold. The first is exclusive to God, that is, to the One who does not receive but only gives; the second belongs to those who receive and give, that is, to men. In other words, God the Son incarnate possesses by nature the plenitude of grace, whereas men receive by grace a participation in this plenitude of Christ, which they can then share with others.

Further distinctions need to be made. Christ's fullness of grace is one thing; that of His divine mother another; that of everyone else, yet another. Firstly, the plenitude of grace in Christ is absolute, whereas the plenitude in Mary is relative to her mission as Mother of God. In other words, her fullness is proportionate to the grandeur of her divine maternity. Accordingly, she possessed from the first moment of her existence a capacity greater than that which all other saints combined possessed at the final moment of their lives; and her capacity grew exponentially throughout her life, so that she went from plenitude to plenitude beyond compare. All other men have a capacity infinitely smaller, so that their fullness of grace, by which they participate in the fullness of Christ, can never compare with that of Our Lady.

Moreover, in the Person of the Son dwells the fullness of divinity and, as incarnate Word, in His body and soul dwell the plenitude of all grace. In the Blessed Virgin, the plenitude of grace dwells in the mind (or the soul) as well as in the womb. In all others it resides only in the soul.

The fullness of grace communicated to the saints is likewise twofold. Firstly, all are given this fullness in such a way as to enable them, through their good works, to cooperate in this fullness, to contribute to the salvation of their neighbor, and to obtain personal salvation. Such a fullness is designated as sufficient, as it suffices for one's eternal salvation. Secondly, there is another fullness communicated to certain souls so that, through good works and through the preaching of the salvific doctrine, they may build up the Mystical Body of Christ, the Church, as a whole. This latter fullness is once again twofold: there is a fullness communicated on the one hand to the Doctors, and, on the other hand, another fullness communicated to the martyrs, as for example in the case of the protomartyr Stephen, of whom it is said that he was "a man full of faith and of the Holy Spirit" (Acts 6:5; cf. 6:8).

Now where is St. Joseph to be situated within this hierarchy of fullness of grace? Fr. Isolani responds as follows: Joseph participates in an *excellent* manner in the fullness of grace of Christ, in a *singular* manner in that of the Blessed Virgin Mary, in a *virtual* manner with regard to that of the apostles, and in a *formal* manner with regard to that of all the other saints.

☘ Joseph partakes in the plenitude of Christ *excellently,* that is, in an eminent manner, to the highest degree possible, by virtue of his paternal and spousal dignity. Indeed, he who merited to be called the father of Our Lord, by virtue of his charity, was granted an exceptional sharing in Christ's plenitude.

༖ Joseph shares in the fullness of Mary, his spouse, *singularly*, that is, in a manner which is unique to him, which is proper to him, above all by virtue of his spousal union with Mary, in addition to his submission and his interior consolations granted by angelic revelation. Without doubt, Joseph alone shared uniquely in the communion of the spiritual and physical joys of his spouse, even those which Mary experienced in her body through the gestation of her son. Joseph and Mary were in fact one.

༖ Joseph participates in the fullness of the apostles, in both mind and body, *virtually*, which means that this fullness exists in potency, though not in actuality. This potency must be understood here in the strongest sense, as that which already contains in essence all the essential conditions of its actualization, even though this does not manifest itself outwardly, just as the acorn contains in itself the essence of the oak. So the plenitude possessed by Joseph is in essence the same as that of the apostles, even though it does not appear outwardly and has not been fully realized in act. For instance, though Joseph has not been ordained to the priesthood as were the apostles, he essentially possesses the sacerdotal graces by virtue of his participation in the divine paternity through his virginal sponsality with Mary and the union with her in the offering of their son.

Joseph participates in the fullness of all other saints *formally*, that is, in actuality, though with an excellence and perfection that do not belong to all the other saints.

Let's now consider more precisely the participation of Joseph in the fullness of grace granted to the apostles. We might be somewhat surprised at first glance, when pondering the notion that Joseph received, in essence, the same plenitude as the apostles. We might very well consider the apostles, due to their zeal and apostolic ministry, as possessing a plenitude essentially superior to that of Joseph, thus having primacy over our humble and silent Carpenter of Nazareth. And yet, with the help of Fr. Isolani, we can envisage not only the equality but even the superiority of Joseph with respect to the holy apostles. The greatness of our saint and of the mission entrusted to him appears in all its splendor if we compare the gifts granted to him with those of the apostles.

Fr. Isolani says that there are four properties of apostolic dignity: (1) the proclamation of the gospel throughout the world (Matt. 28:19); (2) the illumination of the soul (Matt. 5:14: "You are the light of the world"); (3) the reconciliation of sinners with God (Mark 16 and John 20:23: "If you forgive the sins of any, they are forgiven"); and (4) the witness to Christ by means of the Holy Spirit (John 15:26–27). All these properties are most worthy in that they are immediately given to the apostles *by* Christ and are exercised *under* Christ and *through* Him. The properties of the dignity of St. Joseph were likewise fourfold, namely, that he is: (1) spouse of the Queen of Heaven; (2) father of the King of Angels; (3) defender of the Messiah promised in the Law of the Jews; and (4) educator of the Savior of all mankind. These properties are immediately exercised by Joseph *over* Christ, *for* Him, and *through* Him. Note the essential difference between the *under* (on the part of the apostles) and the *over* and *for* (on the part of St. Joseph). Without Joseph's initial and necessary ministry on behalf of the mystery of Christ, there would be no apostolic ministry. From this comparison between St. Joseph and the apostles, there shines forth the uniqueness of the dignity, the holiness, and the virtues of St. Joseph.

When Was St. Joseph Cleansed of Original Sin?

As a corollary to the question of the singular degree of grace granted to St. Joseph in view of his unique mission, there now arises the following question: When was Joseph cleansed of Original Sin? We exclude the idea of his having received the gift of an immaculate conception, for there is neither a revelation nor a constant teaching in this regard. The rite established by the Lord in the Old Testament in order to eliminate Original Sin and to receive grace was circumcision. Grace, however, as St. Paul reminds us in Romans (4:11), was given to Abraham, who received the sign of circumcision not by virtue of circumcision itself but by virtue of the justice received by faith. This faith operated by virtue of the Passion and death of Our Lord by means of circumcision, which was in turn a prefigurative sign of baptism. Grace came from faith signified and not from the justification brought about by circumcision.

St. Joseph was certainly subjected to the rite of circumcision after his birth. Are we to conclude that it was at that moment that he received sanctification by means of grace? The mystical Mother Maria Cecilia Baij, in her *Life of the Glorious Patriarch St. Joseph*, nourished by private revelations that the servant of God had, maintains that circumcision was the moment of Joseph's sanctification. She writes thus, recalling the moment of the circumcision:

> Having been cleansed of the stain which he had contracted
> from original sin, being in the state of grace and friendship

with God, without that stain that would have made him in some manner repugnant to Him, Joseph was adorned by God with many gifts and also with the use of reason, through which Joseph knew his God, and adored Him with profound adoration, bowing his little head, his whole face being illumined.[14]

In a footnote to this text, the editor of the work, Msgr. Pietro Bergamaschi, theologically reinforces this position by referring to St. Thomas Aquinas (*Summa Theologica*, III, q. 27, art. 6). The latter, after having presented the sanctification in the womb on the part of St. John the Baptist (see Luke 1:44) and before him of Jeremiah (Jer. 1:5), adds that it is not to be believed that others have been sanctified in the mother's womb, of which Scripture makes no mention. Such privileges of grace are given to some for the benefit of others. Scripture says nothing about St. Joseph, and it is not even possible to deduce this from a definition of the Magisterium. Therefore, Bishop Bergamaschi concludes that there is none other than John the Baptist whose sanctification in the womb before birth can be affirmed with absolute certainty, and this for the fact that the Precursor found himself confronted with the Redemption that had begun: he was facing Jesus the Redeemer and Mary Co-redemptrix.[15]

However, in accordance with what has been said so far about the singularity of St. Joseph with respect to all the other saints and the superiority of his holiness with respect to John the Baptist, in view of his unique mission as "minister of the divine economy" (to employ the expression of St. Ephrem), it seems reductive to

---

[14] *Vita del glorioso patriarca san Giuseppe*, 1st ed, ed. P. Bergamaschi (1921; repr. Rome: Edizioni Fiducia, 2021), 27–28.

[15] Ibid., n. 3, pp. 26–27.

be forced to exclude a prior sanctification of our holy carpenter simply for the reason that it is not expressly taught by Scripture. If we limit ourselves to the mere data of Scripture, without an adequate interpretation, we should also exclude his superiority with respect to John the Baptist, the greatest among those born of woman (Matt. 11:11 and Luke 7:28). And yet, thanks to Aquinas himself, we have ascertained that in that case, John the Baptist is mentioned as being the last of all those who preceded him in the Old Covenant. Is it not more fitting, and more in conformity with Joseph's vocation, for him to be sanctified in an excellent manner within his mother's womb? Is it not more fitting for him to be sanctified like John the Baptist, and certainly more than him, with superior gifts and virtues, by reason of his mission as spouse of the Mother of God and father of the Son of God? We should, indeed, make room in this discussion for the argument of fittingness.

Many authors, in fact, follow this line of reasoning, beginning with Fr. Isidoro Isolani, in his *summa* on the gifts of St. Joseph. Starting from the fact that Scripture is silent on this fact and that the Magisterium does not teach this doctrine, Fr. Isolani nonetheless offers a series of reasons that can convince us of its veracity.

First, he asserts the fact that every sanctification in the womb happens either because of the excellent future dignity of the sanctified person or because the sanctified person is ordained to Christ, the holy of holies. Joseph excels in both as a "just man."

Second, as Jeremiah was sanctified in his womb by an express prophecy of the coming of Christ, so likewise St. Joseph could be sanctified by an even more explicit proclamation of Christ.

Third, if the sanctification of John the Baptist in his mother's womb is believed by virtue of his being the precursor, why should it not be believed that Joseph's sanctification happened likewise in the womb for the sake of Christ's own education? The capacity comes from Christ Himself. St. Paul, in 2 Corinthians 3:6, writes that Christ "has qualified us to be ministers of a new covenant."[16] In addition to Fr. Suárez and to Gerson, St. Francis de Sales (see *Sermon 25* for the Feast of St. Peter) also defends this theological position.

Finally, St. John Henry Newman, in his *Meditations for the Triduum of St. Joseph*, writes admirably and by way of compendium:

> He is Holy Joseph, because according to the opinion of a great number of doctors, he, as well as St. John Baptist, was sanctified even before he was born. He is Holy Joseph, because his office, of being spouse and protector of Mary, specially demanded sanctity.[17]

---

[16] See ibid., 33.
[17] Newman, *Prayers, Verses, and Devotions*, 322.

Chapter 6

Eternally Preordained to the Hypostatic Order

Having discerned the singular degree of grace granted to Joseph in view of his mission and having demonstrated the fittingness of his sanctification prior to birth, it is fitting likewise for us to now ask ourselves to what order the exceptional mission of St. Joseph belongs. Before venturing an answer to this question, it is necessary first of all to define the concept of "order." It designates the different manners or degrees in which God communicates Himself to man. There are three of them: first of all, the natural order, which is creation; then the supernatural order, which is the gift of sanctifying grace that makes us participants in the divine nature (see 2 Pet. 1:4); and finally, that of the hypostatic union, that is, the communication of the divine nature to the human nature in the Person of the incarnate Word. This is God's supreme degree of communication because this is how God communicated Himself.

The mission of St. Joseph is evidently superior to the order of nature, even of angelic nature. But is his mission simply of the order of grace, as was the case of St. John the Baptist, who prepared the way of salvation, as well as of the apostles, in view of the sanctification of souls in the Church and, more particularly, of the founders of religious orders?

We have just seen that his mission is much greater than the latter. By examining the question carefully, we can see that the mission of St. Joseph goes beyond the order of grace and therefore that of all the saints. Our Saint of Nazareth participates like no other, with the exception of the Virgin Mary, in the order of the hypostatic union, which we have defined in itself as God's maximum participation in human nature and, in this case, the maximum participation of a man in union with God.

Joseph entered into the order of the grace of the Incarnation, which surpasses participation in the supernatural order by means of sanctifying grace, due to the former being the foundation and cause of the latter. His entry into this most special order of grace is realized by his being united to Jesus through a unique task: that of introducing the Son of God into the world in an ordained manner, not through physical generation but through spiritual generation. Through Mary, once again, Joseph comes into contact with the mystery of the incarnate Word and becomes His guardian and minister. The unique grace given to Joseph is well highlighted by St. Bernardine of Siena († 1444), who writes as follows: "Whenever divine grace selects someone to receive a particular grace, or some especially favored position, all the gifts for his state are given to that person, and enrich him abundantly" (*Sermon on St. Joseph*, a. 1).

In what exactly did this grace consist, in order for Joseph to be able to fulfill his mission? St. Bernardine explains it to us again:

A comparison can be made between Joseph and the whole Church of Christ. Joseph was the specially chosen man through whom and under whom Christ entered the world fittingly and in an appropriate way. So, if the whole Church is in the debt of the Virgin Mary, since, through her, it was able to receive the Christ, surely after her, it also owes to Joseph special thanks and veneration. (*Sermon on St. Joseph*, a. 2)

This concept of Joseph as "ordainer" of the birth of Jesus was already very dear to Origen (183–254) who, in his commentary on the Gospel of Luke on the visit of the shepherds, says that they, having gone to Bethlehem "found Joseph, who arranged matters for the Lord's birth (*dispensatorem ortus Dominici*), and Mary, who bore Jesus in childbirth, and the Saviour Himself, 'lying in a manger'" (*Hom. 13 In Lucam*, 7). Thus, Joseph's participation in the mystery of the Incarnation already finds its masterful placement.

The *ordained* insertion of Jesus into the world is a concept taken up by *Redemptoris custos* (no. 8), which comments on Origen's passage as follows:

> Joseph is "the one who has the responsibility to look after the Son of God's "ordained" entry into the world, in accordance with divine dispositions and human laws. All of the so-called "private" or "hidden" life of Jesus is entrusted to Joseph's guardianship.

Joseph is therefore the one who ordains, who gives order to the birth of Jesus and places Him, even if legally, in the Davidic lineage. Joseph ordains the birth of Jesus because he was, in turn, ordained to become one with Mary, and through her, who is the physical mother of Jesus, he enters into the order of God with man: the order of the hypostatic union. It is therefore absolutely essential to see Joseph's participation in this order as subordinate to that of Mary.

By reason of Mary, we understand precisely how and in what manner the participation of her holy spouse is realized. Msgr. Giacomo Sinibaldi (1856–1928), titular bishop of Tiberias and secretary of the Sacred Congregation of Seminaries and Universities, published in 1927 a true masterpiece, *The Greatness of St. Joseph*, in which he examined with precision the question of the participation of the Saint of Nazareth in the order of the hypostatic union. He brought to light the fact that the ministry of St. Joseph belongs to this order in a very precise and specific way: not in the sense that Joseph cooperated intrinsically as a physical instrument of the Holy Spirit in the realization of the mystery of the Incarnation—in this sense his role is far inferior to that of Mary, true Mother of God—but in the sense that he was predestined to be, in the order of moral causes, the protector of Mary's virginity and honor, and at the same time the protector of the incarnate Word. Therefore, his mission belongs, by reason of its finality, to the hypostatic order not through an intrinsic, physical, and immediate cooperation (which solely concerns Mary's cooperation), but through an extrinsic, moral, and mediate cooperation (through Mary), which however is nevertheless a true and real cooperation. Joseph unites himself with his will to Christ and becomes one with Him through Mary, who is instead one with her son by virtue of His will and His flesh. This will have an important implication in Joseph's unique cooperation in the mystery of the Redemption, subordinated only to that of Mary. After Mary there is Joseph, and through Mary, once again, we have all the greatness of Joseph.

This hierarchical approach to the participation of the two holy spouses in the order of the hypostatic union, taken up with its metaphysical distinctions in a recent doctoral thesis on St. Joseph (Giuseppe Attilio Mattanza, "St. Joseph, Head of the

Holy Family in the Papal Magisterium from Pius IX to Our Day," Cantagalli-Eupress FTL, Lugano-Siena, Italy, 2019), in addition to being very precise from the doctrinal point of view, is also very useful from the spiritual one: it teaches us that one goes to God in an orderly way and that one participates in grace in an orderly and hierarchical way. Without Mary and without Joseph with her and for her, there is no possibility for man to participate in divine life through sanctifying grace, emanating from the grace of the incarnate Word, of which Joseph is the *type*. It also teaches us that it is incorrect to level out every distinction in the Church, between the saints in Heaven and the faithful of Christ on earth, in order to say that all are called to holiness and that we are all brothers in Christ. There is a hierarchy in the Church, the Mystical Body of Christ and the communion of saints, even among the saints themselves. In the final analysis, this *hierarchy* underlines the importance of the *mediation* of Christ, Mary, and Joseph in Mary, for our salvation, for obtaining all the graces necessary to attaining it. Any other intercession is conceivable only by respecting this order of the hypostatic union.

Joseph and Mary in the Same Order of Predestination

The singularity and the sublimity of the mission of our saint is further confirmed in the mystery of the eternal predestination of St. Joseph, in one and the same decree with which the Father had foreseen the Incarnation of the Son and the divine maternity of His Immaculate Mother. Joseph, inserted into the same divine order by an act of God's foreknowledge, cannot remain apart. Leo XIII initially reminded us that Joseph "approached nearer than any to the eminent dignity by which the Mother of God surpasses so nobly all created natures" (*Quamquam pluries*, 3), and this by virtue of his marriage with her. Therefore, the great strength of this earthly spousal bond is ultimately rooted in the presence of Joseph with Mary in the same order of predestination.

However, before delving more deeply into this subject it is good to clarify the term *predestination*. In fact, it is easy to confuse this word with "divine providence" or more broadly with "destiny" so as to fall, alas, into a salvific pessimism, where divine arbitrariness would be the background. On the contrary, predestination in its Pauline meaning signifies being inserted into the "design, that is, the plan of God" in which "everything concurs to our good." It is not a question of divine fatality or inevitability but a plan of love that preordains the elect to salvation without taking away their freedom, especially that of being conformed to the image of Christ. The following passage from St. Paul can enlighten us:

> We know that in everything God works for good with those who love him, who are called according to his purpose. For those whom he foreknew he also predestined to be conformed to the image of his Son, in order that he might be the first-born among many brethren. And those whom he predestined he also called; and those whom he called he also justified; and those whom he justified he also glorified. (Rom. 8:28–30)

It is beneficial to begin with this key text, particularly its *incipit*: "We know that in everything God works for good with those who love him, who are called according to his purpose" (Rom. 8:28). Those who are *called* are also *predestined*, that is, destined to be conformed to Christ in everything, so as to be made righteous, that is, sanctified and glorified in Heaven. We find the same teaching in the Letter to the Ephesians, in which it is said that in Christ, the Father "chose us in him before the foundation of the world"

(1:4), and "destined us in love to be his sons through Jesus Christ, according to the purpose of his will" (1:5). Therefore, if we have been chosen from eternity to be sons in the Son, it is first the Son who is elected and *constituted* "first-born among many brethren." The Father sees from eternity the Son who in the fullness of time becomes man and therefore has always preordained the union of the divine nature with human nature in the unique Person of Christ, the incarnate Word (see also *Summa Theologica* III, q. 24, art.1). The Son is thus predestined to the Incarnation, and we, in Him, are likewise predestined to grace and glory.

Through the divine disposing of all things in a most orderly fashion, the Father willed, with Christ and immediately after Him, the Blessed Virgin Mary, foreseen *ab aeterno* as the Immaculate Conception in order to become in time a worthy dwelling place of the Most High, the Mother of God. We may affirm that, immediately after Mary, St. Joseph is "closest" to Christ, by reasoning *sub specie aeternitatis* (in reference to the eternal). Our saint was willed in Christ so that Christ, who was to become incarnate and become man, would thus have an earthly guardian and father. Hence, his predestination to the special mission to which he was called, to be Mary's spouse in order to become the father of the Son of God, precedes that of all other men in grace and glory. The very predestination of St. Joseph to be one with Christ, *pater Verbi* (from the liturgy), precedes his ordination to glory. Fr. Tarcisio Stramare, a great expert on Josephology, points out that John Paul II emphasizes Joseph's paternity rather than sponsality with Mary in relation to the mystery of the Incarnation, in which

> Joseph of Nazareth "shared" [in the Incarnation] like no other human being except Mary, the Mother of the Incarnate Word. He shared in it with her; he was involved in

the same salvific event; he was the guardian of the same love, through the power of which the eternal Father "destined us to be his sons through Jesus Christ" (Eph. 1:5). (*Redemptoris custos*, no. 1)

We should certainly keep in mind both components of the Josephine mystery, the fact of his being, by Mary, and his becoming, through her, the father of the Savior. Yet, as also highlighted by Fr. Réginald Garrigou-Lagrange, all the New Testament indications concord on the fact that St. Joseph was predestined to be the putative father of the incarnate Word before being predestined to glory. The ultimate reason for this is to be found in the fact that the predestination of Christ as man to His divine Sonship precedes the predestination of all the elect, since Christ, as we have said, is the first to be predestined. And as Christ's predestination to the hypostatic union is superior to His predestination to glory and precedes it, and as this same predestination of Mary to be the Mother of God precedes *in signo priori* her predestination to glory, so too the predestination of her most chaste spouse to be father of the Son of God precedes his predestination to glory and to grace. Grace is given in view of glory. In other words, the reason why Joseph was predestined for the highest degree of glory after Mary, and consequently the highest degree of grace and charity, is that he was called to be the worthy foster father and protector of the God-Man.

His being one with Mary, by virtue of virginal sponsality, was aimed at his becoming the Redeemer's father. Christ is the center of the mystery contained in the person of Mary and that of Joseph. Mary and Joseph are chosen from eternity in view of Christ and in dependence upon Him. Sponsality with Mary thus gives way, in the hierarchical order of predestination and therefore of perfection, to the mystery of Joseph's human fatherhood, although the two things are welded together in a mutual relationship. The first chronologically precedes the second and the second is the reason for the first. Therefore, the fact that St. Joseph was predestined by the same decree of the Incarnation shows once again, and in an excellent manner, how lofty his mission was. In conclusion, we can summarize everything as follows: from the singular mission of St. Joseph, preordained from eternity in the same decree of the Incarnation of the Son of God, we can measure the unparalleled greatness of this saint, and thus we go back to the uniqueness of the glory he enjoys in Heaven by reason of the singular grace and charity given to him on earth in order to be faithful to his calling. Joseph after Mary is the most Christlike saint. He, with Mary and through her, conforms us to his son. So let us go to him, let us have recourse to him. The "Ite ad Ioseph" of biblical memory thus finds its firmest and surest expression.

Chapter 7

A Singular Cooperator in the Mystery of Redemption

"How great a share the glorious St. Joseph had in the chalice of Jesus' passion," wrote St. Mary Magdalene de Pazzi, "for the services he rendered to his sacred humanity." His is an exceptional cooperation, though subordinate to that of Mary for the fact that St. Joseph, as we have already mentioned, does not participate in the same way as his spouse in the mystery of the order of the hypostatic union in a physical and intrinsic manner, which belongs only to Mary as Mother of God, but in a moral and extrinsic manner.

St. Joseph's participation in the Redemption is *associative*, by means of Mary, just as Mary in turn is associated with the Redemption in a singular manner by Christ as His immaculate mother. Here, too, there is a divinely ordered hierarchy. However, Joseph unites himself to the salvific work of the Son, not from without but with all his will and with all his fatherly love. In an "extrinsic" manner does not mean from the outside, like a stranger or a spectator, but in a manner that is not physical but rather interior because Joseph did not generate Jesus; likewise, "moral" does not simply mean a good example offered by the Holy

Patriarch but a participation rooted in his heroic charity, in his unique love for Jesus, fruit of a singular grace.

Moreover, his cooperation is not accidental or irrelevant but unique and singular, as is his mission. It embodies the two aspects of the Josephine mystery: the first in relation to the divine motherhood of Mary and by virtue of his virginal marriage with her; the second in relation to Christ, the holy Carpenter of Nazareth being the adoptive father and guardian of the Son of God. Thus, St. Joseph shares in the mystery of our Redemption like no other among all the human creatures, second only to Our Lady from whom he receives, by way of maternal mediation, the capacity to collaborate and by means of whom his collaboration becomes effective. In fact, to Joseph is due the *protodulia*, the special veneration, above all the other saints, inferior to the *hyperdulia* due only to the Virgin Mary, but superior to the *dulia* due to all the other saints.

A True Co-Redemption

Let us now enter into the mystery of this salvific cooperation. A quote from John Paul II from his exhortation on St. Joseph, *Redemptoris custos*, can be of significant help to us:

> St. Joseph was called by God to serve the person and mission of Jesus directly through the exercise of his fatherhood. It is precisely in this way that, as the Church's Liturgy teaches, he "cooperated in the fullness of time in the great mystery of salvation" and is truly a "minister of salvation." (no. 8)

His collaboration is unique because, like that of Our Lady, it takes place during the realization of the Redemption itself, through his being in such close contact with the Redeemer as to become His protector and the "savior" of His life, in view of the final sacrifice of Jesus at Calvary. His collaboration is also active. Joseph, as a "minister of salvation," works with Jesus for us, on our behalf. His consociative work is inscribed by God's will into the universal plan of Redemption. His suffering, the sorrows of his heart, and his sacrificial obedience contribute to our salvation, just as all of Mary's maternal sorrows do. Mary and Joseph—more precisely, Joseph *through* Mary—thus become collaborators of the Most High in the salvation of humanity, in the objective Redemption, so that with them and through them, every man may become an effective cooperator in the mystery of salvation, ready to complete in his flesh what is lacking in Christ's afflictions (Col. 1:24), in subjective Redemption.

For this reason, we can speak in technical terms of a "co-redemption" on the part of St. Joseph, in such a way as to indicate the close relationship between the Redeemer and Joseph, a cooperator with the Redeemer in Mary, who is Co-redemptrix *par excellence.* Joseph's co-redemption derives from Mary's and is subordinate to it. He receives from her a share in her co-redemptive mission. While the Virgin is Co-redemptrix in a *direct* manner, by virtue of her immaculate maternity, Joseph is Co-redeemer in an *indirect* manner, through his marriage with the Blessed Virgin, leading to his salvific paternity. Moreover, the Virgin Mary is Co-redemptrix in an *immediate* manner by reason of her physical bond with Jesus, whereas Joseph is Co-redeemer in a *mediate* manner, through his spouse.

However, both Joseph and Mary play an *active* role in Jesus and with Jesus. They do everything for us; they offer everything for us in Jesus. Doing so in a singular yet hierarchical way, they are now ready to save us from sin and eternal death. They had already received from Christ the grace of salvation in a unique and exceptional way, Mary as the Immaculate Conception, preserved from Original Sin from the moment of her conception and therefore devoid of even the slightest stain of sin; Joseph certainly (at the very least) as sanctified in a very special manner, like John the Baptist, before he was born. Quite rightly then, we can say with Cardinal Alexis-Henri-Marie Lépicier that St. Joseph is the "most perfect coredeemer after Mary."[18]

This most singular cooperation of St. Joseph is confirmed in a magisterial way by Pius XI. In an address delivered in the Consistorial Hall, on March 19, 1928, Pope Pius XI said, after speaking of the missions of St. John the Baptist and St. Peter:

> Between these two missions appears that of St. Joseph, a mission of recollection and silence, a mission almost unnoticed and destined to come to light only many centuries later, a silence that would become a resounding hymn of glory, but only after many years. However, where the mystery is deepest, precisely there the mission is highest, and a more brilliant procession of virtues is required, with their corresponding echo of merits. It was a unique and sublime mission, that of guarding the Son of God, the King of the world, that of protecting Mary's virginity, that of entering into participation in the mystery hidden from the eyes of the world and thus cooperating in the incarnation and redemption.

Moreover, Joseph's work of collaboration was above all necessary to prepare Jesus for the final fulfillment of our salvation, defending Him and leading Him, day after day, to the heights of Golgotha. Just as he will enter silently into the mystery of the

---

[18] *Tractatus de Sancto Josepho: Sponso Beatissimæ Virginis Mariæ*, pt. 2 (Paris, 1908; 3rd ed., Rome, 1933), a. 5, n. 7, p. 208.

God-Man through Mary, so he will silently exit this world, before the fulfillment of the redemptive sacrifice of Our Lord, but only after having entrusted his last paternal collaboration to his spouse, to be taken to Calvary and to be offered by her at that supreme moment.

Joseph's salvific cooperation, unlike Mary's, does not constitute, *stricto sensu*, the "price" of our Redemption, paid by Jesus with His blood and by Mary with her tears and sorrows, and offered once and for all on Golgotha. Yet it is a necessary preparation so that that price might exist and might be offered: it is the *sine qua non* of the Redemption, so that Mary would have a husband and Jesus therefore a father. This enables us to qualify the co-redemption of St. Joseph further, through another distinction. Whereas Jesus is the *principal meritorious cause* of the entirely sufficient and superabundant Redemption, Mary is the *secondary meritorious cause*, dependent on Christ and superabundant by virtue of the unique privilege of grace bestowed upon her by God on our behalf. Joseph, on the other hand, is the *dispositive cause* of the Redemption, that is, he disposes God to intervene. It is necessary here to make an analogy with the Sacrament of the Eucharist. Just as God established that only with matter (bread and wine) and form (the words of consecration) is there the sacrifice of the Mass and sacramental grace, so likewise He established that only thanks to St. Joseph, to his work, his prayer, his guardianship, and his priestly offering, was there the necessary and sufficient condition for the redeeming sacrifice of Jesus and Mary, of the New Adam and the New Eve.

Joseph's Participation in the Priesthood of Christ

After having examined the singular co-redemptive mission of St. Joseph, who was rightly defined by St. John Chrysostom as "minister of salvation" ("Totius dispensationis minister effectus est," *In Matthaeum*, 5, 3), let us move on to examine more deeply the soteriological aspect of his mission, framing it as a participation in the priesthood of Christ. We must remember that all the Lord's disciples share in His high and supreme priesthood, ontologically different from that of Aaron according to the flesh but according to the eternal order of Melchizedech (see Heb. 7:17 in the light of Ps. 110:4).

The Church is a priestly body where the members in an ordered and ontologically distinct way participate in the priesthood of Christ: in such a way as to represent Christ the head and shepherd of the Church in the ministerial priesthood, by virtue of the Sacrament of Holy Orders, and in a common way in the baptismal priesthood, by virtue of the Sacrament of Baptism. As *Lumen gentium* (no. 10) points out, there is not only a difference in degree between these two participations but a substantial difference. The priests are a representation of Christ the priest, head and pastor of His Church, and offer the sacrifice of the Holy Mass *in persona Christi*; and in His Person, they celebrate the other sacraments. The faithful, by virtue of their being inserted into Christ as members of the one Body and under the same Head, *contribute* to the offering of the one sacrifice of the altar, through the offering of their lives and their apostolate, a living sacrifice, holy and pleasing to God (Rom. 12:1). By their holy life and good works, they spread the good fragrance of Christ among men (see 2 Cor. 2:15).

There are therefore two orders of participation in the priesthood of Christ: ministerial and baptismal. Where could we situate St. Joseph? Certainly not among the ministerial priesthood, for he was not ordained a priest by Christ and did not belong to the apostolic college. The simplest solution would be to situate him among the faithful of Christ, therefore as a participant in the common priesthood, although in a *typical* and more elevated manner—since, among the faithful, St. Joseph excels due to his holiness and his unique mission.

However, let us ask ourselves: Would a priesthood common to all the baptized satisfy the uniqueness of the Josephine mystery? Due to the fact that Joseph of Nazareth was not baptized but was sanctified in a very special way—within the maternal womb, as we have affirmed, with the support of various witnesses—and that he belonged to the mystery of the order of the hypostatic union, an order that precedes the Church and the body of the faithful, in such a way as to make him a singular cooperator in the making of the Redemption, we should be able to affirm much more.

The question of the priesthood of St. Joseph now clearly appears to be that of the mode of his participation in the priesthood of Christ and not merely the possibility of his being a priest through the priestly character. The latter could easily be construed if one links the priesthood directly and uniquely to the ordained priesthood rather than to its source, which is the priesthood of Christ. However, Joseph's priesthood must be understood as going hand in hand with the priesthood of Mary, his spouse.

The priesthood of the Mother of God, who was a singular cooperator in the mystery of the Redemption as Co-redemptrix, is unique and cannot be ascribed to either the ordained or the common priesthood, as it rises to a *unique, singular, and superior* degree, as does her unique and singular cooperation in the Redemption. Likewise, Joseph's priesthood should be considered in union with Mary's and subordinate only to it. Like that of his Most Holy Spouse, Joseph's priesthood excels with respect to the priesthood in which all other members of the Church participate, according to the two forms just described, as it is situated on a higher and precedential plane: that of objective redemption, that is, at the very moment of the making of the Redemption and the realization of salvation. The priesthood participated in via the Church, on the other hand, both in its ministerial and in its common form, comes into action at the moment of subjective redemption, that is, of the application of the fruits of salvation to men and this in a sacramental manner.

The priesthood of Christ to which Mary is directly and intimately united as Mother and as New Eve is exercised throughout her life, in all its redemptive mysteries, and its culmination is the offering of the sacrifice of Calvary. There Christ offered Himself in a definitive manner by His death on the Cross. He gave His body and shed all His blood for us, to redeem us from sin and lead us to His Father's kingdom.

To this daily, constant, and sacrificial offering, Mary united herself; *through* Mary, Joseph also participated in this offering. Mary's co-redemption favors Joseph's co-redemption; the priesthood of Mary favors the priesthood of the holy and faithful Nurturer. If our holy and faithful minister of Jesus could hold the Son in his arms and offer Him to the Father for us, it was by means of the virginal motherhood of Mary of which Joseph was the guardian. Thus, he was the guardian of the virginal and maternal sacrifice of his spouse offered for us and for the benefit of the Church in the founding moments of the Church herself. To this sacrifice he joined his own, and he did so in all the redemptive moments of the mysteries of Christ's life in which he was present. As we have already said, at the culminating moment of Golgotha, Joseph was not present, but he had entrusted, before his departure, his final offering to Mary so that she might carry it there on that sacred hill and offer it in his stead.

Moreover, this priesthood of St. Joseph is imbued with uniqueness by the fact that, especially at certain moments of Jesus' life, he is the official protagonist, as father and minister. Let us think, for example, of the circumcision of the Child, eight days after His birth (Luke 2:21). It was he, as a father, who had to make that cut in the flesh of the Son, and it was he who therefore offered that first redemptive blood for the salvation of mankind. Joseph had learned from the angel that it was for him, as father, to give the name "Jesus" to the Child: "for he will save his people from their sins" (Matt. 1:21). That name imposed at the moment of the circumcision thus began to produce its first salvific effects. That first drop of blood that the father collected during that rite, together with his spouse, was adored and offered to the Father in Heaven as a pledge of eternal salvation—a highly priestly gesture that teaches all priests how to offer the Body and Blood of the Son on the altar.

In the presentation of the Child Jesus in the temple, the Guardian of the Redeemer also played a special role. The Gospel text in this case does not introduce a significant difference between Mary and Joseph who "brought him up to Jerusalem to present him to the Lord ... and to offer a sacrifice according to what is said in the law of the Lord, 'a pair of turtledoves, or two young pigeons'" (Luke 2:22–24). One can imagine in these moments Joseph's role, the disposition of his soul in the offering, fully aware of the mystery that was being fulfilled and in which he had been called to collaborate. This is the "morning offering" as described by St. Bernard, in which St. Joseph takes part in a singular manner and which will be a prelude to the "evening offering" of Calvary, already fulfilled here *as a vow* and with all the love of his heart. Just as Abraham is a figure of Joseph, by preparing the lamb and with a priestly action preparing to sacrifice him, but without actually being the one to do so, so Joseph is, in some way, a "figure" of Mary, of the one who, being *one* with Christ, sacrificed Jesus and with Jesus *sacrificed* herself. He is a "figure" because he receives his priesthood from Christ through Mary and always exercises it by means of Mary, like Abraham and more than Abraham, as the latter in reality is *a type* of Mary and of her sacrificial offering. Isaac's question to his father, Abraham, "Behold, the fire and the wood; but where is the lamb for a burnt offering?" (Gen. 22:7), was answered by Joseph even before John the Baptist: "Here is the Lamb of God who takes away the sins of the world. My son, whom I hold in my hands and see with my eyes, is this Lamb."

In 1866 there was a *postulatum* to the Holy See in order to insert the name of St. Joseph in the Roman Canon by Fr. Francesco Maria Cirino, canon regular and consultor of the Sacred Congregation of Rites. As we know, the request was granted only with the reform of the Missal of 1962. However, it is important to highlight the theological reasons offered by Fr. Cirino that motivated such a request. They were based on the fact that Joseph of Nazareth participated in a singular way in the life of the high priest and victim Himself, deducing that it was

> absolutely worthy that *infra Actionem*, in which the Holy Eucharist is realized, the name of Joseph not be silenced, since for many years he sweated and caught cold night and day in the cultivation of this Wheat of the elect.[19]

Moreover, according to Fr. Cirino, our Joseph,

> "although he was not a priest, nevertheless exercised in some way the offices towards the Most Holy Body of

---

[19] Quoted in Tarcisio Stramare, *San Giuseppe: Fatto religioso e teologia* (Camerata Picena, Italy: Shalom, 2018), p. 511, our translation.

the Child Jesus." This was already the case in the rite of circumcision, where "the Lord Jesus gave to the world, *through Joseph's hands*, the first fruits of that most holy blood which he was to shed in remission of sins, and Joseph offered them at the beginning most devoutly to God the Father as a pure oblation and a pleasing host." In the temple, then, "it goes without saying that the most important role is incumbent upon St. Joseph as father; and therefore he himself, with his own hands, fully aware of the mysteries, not only ceremonially, but with all the strength of his soul, presented the child Jesus, the true victim of the holocaust, the salvific sacrifice of Judah and of Jerusalem, which was to be consumed on the altar of the Cross; Joseph himself offered this victim and consecrated him to God the Father on the altar of the temple."[20]

On the basis of these priestly arguments, Fr. Cirino, joined by Fr. Stramare, finds it not only just, pious, and permissible that in the Canon there be the commemoration of St. Joseph but also that this great saint be proposed "as an example and special patron of priests."[21] Just as St. Joseph knew how to guard the Child Jesus in his holy hands and carry Him respectfully, so His priests must learn to serve at the altar with purity of heart and innocence of action, worthily offering and receiving the Most Holy Body and Blood of Christ.[22] Truly in this way, and with a clear priestly connection to Christ's priesthood, St. Joseph becomes a model for all the faithful, and for priests in particular.

---

[20] Quoted in ibid., 514–515, our translation.
[21] Quoted in ibid., 515.
[22] See ibid.

His ministering *coram Deo*, his being night and day in the presence of Christ and at His service, becomes an incentive for every priest to put at the center the adoration of the holy mysteries, the adoration of Christ. Joseph's priestly fatherhood also becomes an icon of priestly fatherhood. His fatherhood is seasoned with virginity and chastity because it is the guardian of the truth of the Word, of His having been conceived by the power of the Holy Spirit. The fatherhood of the priest cannot prescind from his celibacy, which is not a mere law which excludes marriage, but is the expression of a total love for Christ in defense of His holy Incarnation through the Virgin Mary by means of the Spirit of God. The Holy Spirit directs the life of the priest and has primacy in everything so that he may belong entirely to Christ, just like His holy parent. The priest must become a saint like Joseph, who, according to Jacob of Sarug (ca. 451–521), "was as pure, as holy, and as spiritual as Melchizedech, and who became a priest to minister to the Lord of holiness" (*Homily on the Nativity of the Lord*, prose translation of v. 207).

Chapter 8

Figure of the Bridegroom and Minister of the Bread of Life

Both timely and timeless are these words of Jacob of Sarug, celebrating the holiness and the purity of Joseph in the exercise of his priestly ministry with regard to his son, as in this respect he serves as a model for priests of all times, and most especially of this our time. The exemplarity of his priestly ministry is also revealed in a typological theme which was dear to the Fathers of the Church—namely, that Joseph is a type of the heavenly Bridegroom as he is chastely united to Mary, in the same way as Christ is united to the Church. The same is also true of bishops, and therefore of priests, who are likewise espoused to the Church.

Let us delve now into this theme, to see another facet of Joseph's role as model for priests. St. Ambrose provides a sketch of this theme, which is then developed by other Fathers, who highlight the figure of St. Joseph as the spouse of Mary in relation to Christ the Bridegroom of the Church. The holy bishop of Milan focuses on this theme in detail in order to develop the parallels between the virginal maternity of Mary and that of the Church.

Both Mary and the Church are married virgins. As Mary is married to Joseph, so the Church is espoused to Christ. Therefore, as St. Ambrose writes, Joseph's virginal and fruitful marriage with Mary represents that of Christ with the Church:

> We have learnt the order of events; we have learnt the purpose of these events. But let us also learn the mystery. It is good that Mary is both a wife and a virgin, for she is a figure of the Church who is without stain (*immaculata*) (cf. *Ep* 5:27), and yet a spouse. As a virgin (the Church) has conceived us by the Spirit; as a virgin she brings us forth without the pangs of labour. There may, too, be another reason why Holy Mary became fruitful by One (the Holy Spirit) who was not her husband (Joseph), for the individual churches — made fruitful by the Holy Spirit (cf. *Rv* 2:17) and by grace — are visibly united to a mortal bishop. (*Exposition of the Gospel*, 2, 6)

As can be seen, the Ambrosian reference is to the particular churches at the head of which there is a bishop. There is no reference to the text of Ephesians (5:25–32) that concerns the union of Christ with the Church, His Body made holy and immaculate. Therefore, the Josephine reference would seem more suitable as a veiled sign of the model of the bishops, spouses of the churches, and therefore of the priests, spiritual pastors of the Church.

St. Paulinus of Nola (355–431), although not expressly naming St. Joseph, is the first who, in one of his poems, addresses the theme of the Christo-ecclesiological typology of the marriage between Joseph and Mary, with a clear reference to Ephesians (5:32). Here is the relevant passage:

> Without intercourse, a woman's womb conceived new life. This bride did not submit to a mere human husband. She was a mother and bore a child without the woman's role in intercourse. The compact made her a spouse, but she was

no wife in body. She became the mother of a Boy though she was untainted by a husband. What a great mystery was this, by which the Church became wedded to Christ and became at once the Lord's bride and His sister! The bride with the status of spouse is a sister because she is not subject … She is sister and spouse because her intercourse is not physical but mental, and her Husband is not man but God." (*Poem 25, vv.* 161–173, translation into prose of the Latin verse)

Then another Father, St. Peter Chrysologus, took up this theme and broadened it with reference to the Church as fruitful virginal spouse of the bishop who embodies the figure of Joseph, spouse of Mary. The holy bishop of Ravenna, preaching on the day of Marcellin's episcopal consecration, says the following:

She who bore him (the Church of Ravenna) is, in addition, a bride; she is both a mother and a virgin; and she marvels with a new kind of rejoicing that she produced him in the very marriage-bed of her Bridegroom, in the very bedroom of her union. But let it disturb no one, let it trouble no one that in that very marriage-bed we see that the Bride herself has given birth: this kind of conception derives not from anything blameworthy, but from virginity, since in this kind of offspring the birth is heavenly rather than human in origin; there is no place here for evil suspicions, where the Bridegroom himself is on hand as the witness and guardian of his Bride. Whoever among you has been anxious about this matter, may an example put you completely at ease; and may the worry felt by a figure in the past provide you with a sense of security and confidence. That is, Joseph, who was a husband in name only, a spouse in his conscience, was confused and troubled when he saw that his fiancée was pregnant, in that he could neither accuse her in her innocence nor find an excuse for her being pregnant. It was unsafe to keep silent, but it was dangerous to speak. The accuser of one who is innocent commits rather than reveals a crime. He himself was the proof of her chastity, the guardian of her purity: he knew one thing, but what was before his eyes was something very different; what he saw confused him, while the Virgin's fidelity gave him no cause for confusion … And what did the angel say? "Joseph, have no fear." Did the one who had not done anything have to fear? He was fearful because although there was not any guilt regarding any action on his part, there was the greatest amount of terror regarding the situation. Whatever a holy mind does not comprehend causes terror. (*Sermo 175, De Marcellino episcopo et de Virginis partu*)

St. Peter Chrysologus, in addition to outlining this typological spousal parallelism on the basis of the particular church and the bishop placed at its head, goes further. He establishes for the first time a new typological relationship between Joseph of Egypt sold by his brothers and Joseph of Nazareth, both prefiguring in a perfective way—the second reuniting in himself the qualities of the first—Christ in His Passion, spouse of the Church. Thus, it appears that Joseph of Nazareth is properly a figure of Christ the Bridegroom—he is "spouse on behalf of another"—preceding Him temporally and delineating in his person the redemptive traits that will be proper to the Son in relation to the Church. Here is the text:

Why is the secret design of celestial purity fulfilled in a married woman rather than in a free one?… We know that in the gospel neither accents, nor letters, nor syllables, nor nouns, nor persons are void of signification. There is need here of a bride to symbolize the Church, bride of Christ.... And she is truly the spouse, she who, through a virginal birth, gives a new bride back to Christ. Joseph is married on behalf of another, to complete the figure of the passion of Christ in the ancient Joseph. (*Sermo* 146, *De Ioseph sponso, et sponsa matre*)

Here, as we have said, the typological relationship that unites Joseph of Nazareth to Jesus, both of them being spouses, is stitched together starting from Joseph sold by his brothers and becoming prime minister of Egypt (see Gen. 37–50). The first Joseph is an eminent figure of Christ, and Chrysologus highlights the traits he shares in common with Christ. Just as Joseph in his prophetic dreams incurred the zeal of the brethren, so Christ in His prophetic visions aroused envy. As Joseph, enclosed in a cistern, reemerged alive, so Christ, enclosed in the tomb after His death, came out alive. Joseph was sold, and the price agreed upon was Christ; as Joseph was taken to Egypt, likewise Christ had to find refuge from Herod in Egypt. To the people in need in time of famine, Joseph provided bread abundantly, just as Christ is the Bread that comes down from Heaven to feed all nations.

Thus, only after having outlined this Christological typology of the ancient Joseph, Chrysologus introduces the discourse relating to our Joseph of Nazareth: "Thus it appears that Joseph anticipated the type of this heavenly bridegroom (*iste coelestis sposi typum praetulerit*), whose image he bore (*portaverit imaginem*), of whose life his own was the figure (*ambulaverit in figuram*)" (*Sermo* 146, *De Ioseph sponso, et sponsa matre*). The holy carpenter is a figure of Christ, ultimately because the ancient Joseph is a figure of the new Joseph, and the latter finally introduces the reality of which he, too, is a figure by virtue of his being spouse: Christ. A truly wonderful interweaving that binds the Old and New Testaments in the mystery of Christ's Passion and death.

Moreover, if, in the words of Aphraates (one of the most ancient Syriac authors, known as the "Persian Sage"), "Joseph who was persecuted was a type of the persecuted Jesus" (*Demonstration* 21.9), then the first Joseph is linked to the second precisely by virtue of the Passion of Christ. Joseph of Nazareth is therefore a type of the heavenly Bridegroom because he unites himself in a chaste way to Mary, in the same way as Christ is united to the Church; he flees to Egypt to preserve the life of the little infant: if the latter had died prematurely, He would not have achieved what He had come for. Finally, he was minister not of wheat to be distributed in abundance but of the Bread of Life itself. He immediately preceded Christ and therefore introduced Him into His sorrowful Passion with his ministerial and paternal action. In this sense, Joseph is properly "spouse on behalf of another" (*procurator Ioseph sponso*). This is then yet another theme that highlights the unique participation in the Redemption of St. Joseph, who has now been clearly outlined as a Christological figure.

St. Joseph, Minister of the Holy Eucharist

Holy Joseph was the minister of the Bread of Life, having been prefigured by the ancient Joseph who had served as the minister of wheat in Egypt. Clearly, Joseph was the minister of Jesus, the Bread from Heaven, serving Him through his paternal and providential care of the Child. This ministry of fatherly service which Joseph rendered throughout his life with Jesus leads us to ponder the following question: Did Jesus reveal to St. Joseph His desire to institute the Holy Eucharist? Might He have done so during the years of His hidden life in Nazareth? Or perhaps before the beginning of His public life, that is, before Joseph fell asleep in God?

It is not easy to answer this question, nor is it easy to extract some clues from the Gospel accounts. Let us try, however, to investigate the issue rationally, by admitting and having recourse to the central theological principle of fittingness. It was certainly fitting for Jesus to reveal to the one who, after Mary His Mother, was closest to Him, the secret of secrets, the love of His Heart, the desire of all desires: the Holy Eucharist. In the Gospel of Luke (22:15), Jesus, employing a truly singular and paradigmatic construction, says the following: "Desiderio desideravi hoc pascha manducare vobiscum antequam patiar." Literally, this also recalls the original Greek form that follows the same construction, where the verb "to desire" and the noun "desire" are linked so as to re-inforce one another. He is thus saying: "I have desired with great desire to eat this Passover with you before suffering."

We can well imagine that this great desire animated Jesus from His earliest years and that He therefore did not hold back His heart from confiding it to Mary, His mother, and then to Joseph His father. It must have been this "eucharistic desire" that, having been confided to Joseph, motivated our saint in a very special way to become one with the Son and with his spouse. This desire manifests itself especially in his being always generous in the offering of himself—an offering of desire and love—so that all men might be saved. If, according to St. Augustine, desire is the "thirst of the soul," and if, according to St. Thomas Aquinas, *desiderium ex amore*, to desire one must love, hence "Amor praecedit desiderium," love precedes desire.

Therefore, St. Joseph must have—at the very least—shared, by virtue of his love, that thirst of his son's Heart and with Him desired what He desired. However, it is also very fitting to suppose that Jesus revealed to him His intention to institute the Blessed Sacrament, the Love that precedes all desire.

Joseph indeed wanted to become Eucharist with Jesus and Mary. Like his Spouse, he conformed himself to that mystery with his desire, even before it was instituted. His was a communion of love and desire, of love that, being the soul of desire, sets love on fire, a spiritual communion lived with Jesus throughout his life, which was intertwined with Mary's spiritual communion so as to become a desire for oblation in Jesus. Joseph, like Mary, made the sacrificial dimension of the Eucharist his own. His life was a daily preparation for the sacrifice of Calvary, at which he was absent, but after having already arranged everything: he handed over to his Spouse his oblative contribution, his paternal price, asking her to carry it in his stead up the mount of the Crucifixion. Joseph entrusted to Mary all his desire to be one with Jesus, in her and through her, so as to become *one single host* with Jesus. The following passage from John Paul II's encyclical on the Eucharist, *Ecclesia de Eucharistia* (no. 56), could apply not only to Mary but also to Joseph:

> Mary, throughout her life at Christ's side and not only on Calvary, made her own *the sacrificial dimension of the Eucharist.* When she brought the child Jesus to the Temple in Jerusalem "to present him to the Lord" (*Lk* 2:22), she heard the aged Simeon announce that the child would be a "sign of contradiction" and that a sword would also pierce her own heart (cf. *Lk* 2:34–35). The tragedy of her Son's crucifixion was thus foretold, and in some sense Mary's *Stabat Mater* at the foot of the Cross was foreshadowed. In her daily preparation for Calvary, Mary experienced a kind of "anticipated Eucharist"—one might say a "spiritual communion"—of desire and of oblation, which would culminate in her union

with her Son in his passion, and then find expression after Easter by her partaking in the Eucharist which the Apostles celebrated as the memorial of that passion.

It would be enough to exchange in this passage the name "Mary" with that of "Joseph" to have the same result, with the exception of Joseph's participation in the Holy Mass celebrated by the apostles. Joseph made *the sacrificial dimension of the Eucharist* his own through Mary.

In the temple, he is next to his spouse and hears Simeon's words, which become a sword also to his Heart. Those prophetic words, "This child is set for the fall and rising of many in Israel, and for a sign that is spoken against (and a sword will pierce through your own soul also), that thoughts out of many hearts may be revealed" (Luke 2:34–35), cannot but pierce his soul as well as, though he finds himself utterly helpless at the culminating moment of the "fall and rising of many," he nonetheless completely resigns himself to the Father's will.

He prepares day after day for Calvary. He knows that he will not be there physically, but he is always there, in desire, where the Son and where his spouse are. The more love grows, the more desire grows. Joseph experiences Calvary throughout his life, as the ultimate preparation for his spiritual Calvary, for the Eucharist which he receives as a spiritual gift of a love consummated until his death. Joseph perceives the Eucharist, lives it out day after day, adores it, and conforms himself to it in that which is most proper to it: its sacrificial dimension. *Desire and offering* go always together and are one in the life of our Holy Patriarch.

Fr. Tarcisio Stramare adds another eucharistic pearl to the mystery of St. Joseph. His reflection begins with Joseph being sold by his brothers, who providentially, during a period of famine in

Israel, became prime minister of the Pharaoh of Egypt and was able to provide bread for his brothers. When the famine was also felt in Egypt, Pharaoh ordered the Egyptians: "Go to Joseph; what he says to you, do" (Gen. 41:55). The famine then raged throughout the world, but Joseph, as a good *minister*, was able to provide not only for Egypt but also for all the people of the earth. The text adds:

> So when the famine had spread over all the land, Joseph opened all the storehouses, and sold to the Egyptians, for the famine was severe in the land of Egypt. Moreover, all the earth came to Egypt to Joseph to buy grain, because the famine was severe over all the earth. (Gen. 41:56–57)

Joseph of Egypt is just one figure of our Joseph, true minister of the Son of God and dispenser of the true wheat, the true bread, of Jesus Himself. Fr. Stramare reflects on the gesture of "breaking bread," which is then set on the table, performed many times by Joseph at home and in front of Jesus. The bread that Joseph broke was "for" Jesus. But Jesus was also aware that He Himself was that "broken bread." Fr. Stramare writes:

> Joseph foresaw this in his innermost self, although he did not know how much or how. He had sensed it in the words addressed to Mary on the occasion of the presentation of Jesus in the temple: "A sword will pierce your soul too" (*Lk* 2:35). He had feared it in his hasty flight to Egypt to avoid Herod's murderers. He had suffered it in the anguished (v. 48) search for Jesus who had remained in the temple, where the twelve-year-old had replied: "Why were you seeking me? Did you not know that I must be about my Father's business?" … What may then be said of St. Joseph's sentiment of adoration towards the divine Presence, which was

already revealed in his decision to leave his spouse, who was recognized as being "with child by the Holy Spirit" (Mt 1:18), and then expressed at the moment of Jesus' birth, when he was the first to hold him in his arms, making of his entire existence a sacrifice, through paternal love?[23]

This enlightening thought, which finds support in the preference for the thesis of St. Joseph's humility before the mystery of the Incarnation, is also expressed by the eucharistic saint Peter Julian Eymard, who describes it as follows:

> [Joseph] penetrated, so to speak, the coarse garment of Jesus: his faith penetrated the Sacred Heart and, illuminated by the divine light, he foresaw all the states through which Jesus would pass, and he adored them and united himself to the grace of those mysteries. He adored Jesus in his hidden life; he worshipped him in his passion and death; he worshipped him even then in the Holy Tabernacle. Could Our Lord have hidden anything from St. Joseph? The holy Patriarch therefore received the grace of all the states of Jesus, including that of adoring the Blessed Sacrament, ours.[24]

The holy carpenter is a "minister of the Eucharist" because he prepared Jesus to "break the bread"—to break Himself, His Body—for us, by offering him the example of his daily and indomitable sacrifice. In his offering, Joseph worshipped his son's offering, and united himself with it, becoming one with Mary and through Mary, one thing, one heart. With his heart, *in desiderio*, Joseph adored Jesus, the "broken bread," and he already perceived the mystery that the

---

[23] Stramare, *San Giuseppe: Fatto religioso*, 512–514.
[24] Ibid., 514.

Son would institute on the night He was betrayed. Thus, he is our model of adoration of the Holy Eucharist. The exhortation, "Ite ad Ioseph" – "Go to Joseph" – thus finds its proper foundation.

His Final Privilege: A Happy Death and Resurrection

Joseph, as we have seen, prepared day after day for Calvary. Knowing he would not be physically present, he thus confided his own oblative desire to his spouse, so that with her own sacrifice would be joined that of her beloved Joseph. Having experienced Calvary throughout his life, Joseph joined his co-redemptive offering to that of his son and his spouse, thus meriting two very special privileges at the close of his holy life, as we will now see.

Thus, as we near the end our Josephine journey of theological reflection, whose goal was to perceive the greatness of a saint who, after the Blessed Virgin Mary, has no equal, and before ending with the devotional fruit borne of this reflection, it is right and just that we dwell on the two final privileges of St. Joseph. Many saints, blesseds, and various writers have bestowed on our humble carpenter the final privilege of a happy death and resurrection.

First of all, there is the privilege of his happy death. Due to the fact that, from the beginning of Jesus' public life, Joseph no longer appears alongside the Redeemer, it is reasonable to suppose that he had already died and that his death was therefore quite special due to the presence of Jesus and Mary. In fact, the privilege of his blessed passing allows us to contemplate Joseph in the arms of Jesus and Mary, who is consumed with love for her God.

Many confraternities of the happy death, of the dying, of the pious passing of our saint have come into being over the centuries. I would like to mention two of the more recent ones. In

Rome, at the Basilica of St. Joseph on the Triumphal Way, Pius XI established the Pious Union of St. Joseph for the Salvation of the Dying on February 13, 1913. This union was founded by St. Louis Guanella.

Going further south, Bl. Bartolo Longo, a great devotee of the Holy Rosary and founder of the Basilica of Our Lady of Pompeii, who was very devoted to St. Joseph, committed himself to promoting this devotion, so that the Holy See would grant the liturgical celebration of the Passing of St. Joseph to be celebrated on the twentieth of July. In 1890, he dedicated an altar to his passing in the Basilica of Pompeii, erecting at the same time the Pious Union of the Dying under the Patronage of St. Joseph, of which Pope Leo XIII was the first member.

Benedict XV, with the Motu Proprio *Bonum sane* of July 25, 1920, recommended to pastors to make known, among the various associations, those dedicated to St. Joseph in favor of the dying, for the fact that this great saint "is deservedly considered as the most effective protector of the dying, having passed away with the assistance of Jesus and Mary." The Litany of St. Joseph also mentions his important role in three invocations: *Hope of the sick, Patron of the dying,* and *Terror of demons.*

Then, there is Joseph's ultimate great privilege: his resurrection at the moment of Jesus' death and therefore his entry into Heaven with his body as well. The subject becomes a little more difficult with regard to this privilege because, though it is an opinion expressed by some eminent saints and theologians, it nonetheless has no support in Tradition or in Scripture. Therefore, we can speak more precisely of a "possible" privilege. It is a pious belief that requires "devotional faith." It would seem somewhat rash to deny it outright, but at the same time it is hard to affirm it with certainty. So, we must leave the final word to divine providence and its inscrutable plans. It is, however, our task to endeavor to better understand the significance of this possible privilege.

The Gospel text from which the explanation of this privilege stems is Matthew 27:52–53. At the death of Jesus, the veil of the temple was torn in two, rocks were split, the earth shook, and "the tombs also were opened, and many bodies of the saints who had fallen asleep were raised, and coming out of the tombs after his resurrection they went into the holy city and appeared to many." Among these dead who rise should undoubtedly be found our Joseph. After Pierre Pocquet († 1405) and Gerson († 1429), the first to preach it in a heartfelt way was the Franciscan St. Bernardine of Siena († 1444) who, in his *Sermon on St. Joseph*, writes as follows:

> We may piously believe, but not assert, that the Most Holy Son of God, Jesus, crowned his foster-father with the same privilege which he gave his Mother: that as he assumed her into heaven bodily and gloriously in soul, so also on the day when he arose, he took Joseph up with him in the glory of the Resurrection. So that, just as this glorious family, Christ, the Virgin and Joseph, had dwelt together on earth in the labours of life and in loving grace, so now they reign in heaven in loving glory of both body and soul.

St. Bernardine was joined by two other Franciscans, Bl. Bernardine of Feltre († 1494) and Bl. Bernardine de Bustis († 1513). In the sixteenth century, another incomparable preacher of this pious privilege was the Dominican Isidore of Isolanis, whom we have already encountered, author of the first synthesis of the graces granted to St. Joseph, among which there is also that of *the glorification of Joseph in body and soul.*

According to Fr. Isolanis, who supports his thesis thanks to Matthew 27:52–53, among the dead who rise from the tombs at the moment of Christ's death, there is St. Joseph, and he gives various reasons for this. If this privilege was given to those saints by reason of the excellence of their holiness, and as Joseph's holiness was second to none, then quite rightly the privilege of bodily resurrection must have been accorded to him as well. Moreover, it would seem disrespectful if the Son had not honored His father, tolerating that his mortal body remain in the dust.

Another reason of fittingness is identified by Fr. Isolanis: the care that Jesus had for His mother after His Resurrection. Mary Most Holy was the first to be consoled by the Risen Jesus because she had suffered much with Him. It was only just that St. Joseph, who had raised Him, should also be consoled likewise. Perhaps Joseph was one of the risen dead who appeared to many; perhaps he appeared even to the Blessed Virgin. The evangelists, says Fr. Isolanis, omitted to write these things for a prudential reason, just as they did not transmit the fact that the mother was the first witness of the Resurrection of the Son.

The Spanish theologian Francisco Suárez (1548–1617) also supported this thesis, which would later be adopted by St. Francis de Sales. Closer to us, we find the position of Cardinal Alexis-Henri-Marie Lépicier, who uses the adverb *probabiliter* to explain, with the help of many serious authors, that St. Joseph was among those saints whom Christ resurrected to eternal life and whom He took with Him to Heaven.

Even Pope St. John XXIII, very devoted to St. Joseph, became the spokesman of this pious belief in his homily for the canonization of St. Gregory Barbarigo, pronounced on May 26, 1960, in which he links the text recounting the Ascension of Jesus into Heaven with Matthew 27:52–53, saying that the honor and privilege of inaugurating this wonderful accompaniment of the Lord into Heaven belongs to the deceased of the Old Testament. Among these deceased, the pope expressly names John the Baptist, the forerunner, and Joseph of Nazareth, the nurturer.

In this matter, one must avoid being either rash in denying or certain in asserting. However, nothing prevents us, in our devotion, from piously believing in this privilege while leaving the final judgment to the inscrutable mystery of divine election and predestination. In any case, the greatness of St. Joseph is certainly enriched by it, being now suffused with an aspect that far exceeds our *intellectus fidei*.

Model Worker, Mighty Intercessor

In this magnificent painting, the great Spanish artist Murillo depicts both profound theological truths and touching familial tenderness. Let us briefly contemplate this artwork as it can help us perceive how Joseph, through Mary, plays an important role in our lives.

It shows God the Father in Heaven and God the Son on earth, united by the dove of the Holy Spirit, thus forming the Celestial Trinity on the vertical axis of the composition. The Child Jesus has His eyes turned heavenward, but at the same time he affectionately holds the hands of His two parents, the Virgin Mary on His right and St. Joseph on His left, thus forming, on the horizontal axis, what can be called, analogically, the earthly trinity. This analogy possesses a twofold signification: whereas the Child Jesus, of course, represents who He is in Person, the Son of God, Joseph and Mary can both be seen as representing the two other Persons of the Holy Trinity. The primary interpretation, with regard to Mary, is that she represents the Father, as St. John Eudes explains:

This marvellous Mother bears within herself a perfect likeness of the first Person of the Most Holy Trinity ... [who] communicates to her in a most eminent degree his highest perfection, which is his eternal Fatherhood ... To say that the Virgin Mother is a living and very accomplished image of the Father of Jesus, and that she is clothed with his adorable fecundity, his divine virtue, his amiable fatherhood, is to declare emphatically that her sacred Heart bears within itself a very excellent likeness of those same perfections of the Father of Jesus, who, as he communicates so excellently his eternal Fatherhood to the maternal Heart of the most precious Virgin, also communicates to her the infinite love he bears for his Son and the indescribable zeal he has for his glory. (*The Admirable Heart of the Most Sacred Mother of God*, bk. 5, chap. 9)

A secondary interpretation consists in seeing the Blessed Virgin, Spouse of the Holy Spirit, as being the "quasi-incarnation" of the third Person of the Most Holy Trinity, to use the expression of St. Maximilian Kolbe. Or, to put it once again in the words of this great Polish saint, she can be seen as the created Immaculate Conception, visible presence on earth of the uncreated Immaculate Conception, the Holy Spirit in Heaven. As sanctifying grace is the gift of the Holy Spirit, who makes us holy and immaculate before Him in love, so Mary is the means by which all graces come to us. Our Lady is the necessary Mediatrix as she is indissolubly united with the giver of grace. The only way to be imbued with the Holy Spirit is indeed to be united with His holy spouse.

No one could ever be more intimately united with Mary than Joseph, so much so that he, through Mary, bears within himself the perfect likeness of both the Holy Spirit and the Father. As Mary and Joseph are but one, what can be said of Mary can likewise be said, though to a lesser degree, of her holy spouse. By virtue of his oneness of will with his spouse, he was granted a singular degree of sanctification, greater than all saints excepting Mary.

Therefore, Joseph, through his perfect union with Mary, can be seen as representing her heavenly Spouse, the Holy Spirit. He is our model and means for being imbued with the Holy Spirit by means of Mary. We go to Mary through Joseph, and through Mary to the Holy Spirit. Through his espousal with Mary, he also bears within his soul the likeness of the Father, clothed as he is in spiritual fecundity and virginal fatherhood. St. Joseph therefore can be seen as representing God the Father by making visible His benevolent providence. Joseph, who is united as father to Jesus through Mary, leads us along the same royal pathway: *ad Jesum per Mariam*. This is why, in this lovely painting, while Mary gazes lovingly at her Child, St. Joseph turns his gaze upon us, inviting us to kiss the hand of the Child Jesus and to welcome Him into our own lives.

Espousing the pious belief that Joseph was raised, body and soul, into Heaven, enables us to envision this great saint by the side of Jesus and Mary, as he was on this earth, united as the earthly trinity, icon of the heavenly Trinity. We envision his enthronement in Heaven where—after having prefigured Christ as Bridegroom of the Church, after having served as minister of the Holy Eucharist in the Person of the incarnate Son—he now acts as guardian of Holy Mother Church and her greatest treasure, our eucharistic Lord. We see him by Jesus' side, continuing to exercise his co-redemptive priesthood alongside the Eternal High Priest, always through the mediation of Mary.

We perceive Joseph's place in the life of the Church, and thus in our own life, as our life is lived according to the rhythm of the liturgical year and is sustained by our daily bread, the Eucharist, given to us this day and every day.

From this supernatural vantage point, we also perceive St. Joseph's role in our workaday life; just as his humble labor as craftsman of Nazareth possessed a co-redemptive meaning, so likewise do our own laborious activities take on a co-redemptive significance. We sense his presence in our spiritual life, guiding us in our personal growth, his mediatorial role always exercised through Mary.

We go to Joseph, who takes us by the hand to Mary, his Spouse, who takes us to her son, Our Lord and Savior. Indeed, Joseph is our model in our Marian devotion as he was the first to be totally consecrated to her, so as to be totally consecrated to God.

In this final section, we will first consider Joseph as guardian of the Mystical Body of Christ, before reflecting on his presence in our personal life, in our day-to-day work as well as in our life of prayer and devotion.

Chapter 9

Joseph in the Life of the Church

St. Joseph is the treasurer of the Most High. In fact, God entrusts Himself into his hands. Jesus gives Himself to Joseph by becoming his son. For this to happen, the Son gives him first of all His most precious possession, the Immaculata, the one who would shortly thereafter become His mother.

In Mary, Joseph binds himself forever to Jesus. His whole being is now all for Jesus. Mary acts as a Mediatrix between Christ and Joseph. Joseph's sponsality with Mary grafts the holy Carpenter of Nazareth into the mystery of Redemption and makes him an active participant in salvation so that Joseph truly collaborates in it, thus becoming the very model of every Christian, called to become a collaborator with God in his own salvation as well as that of others. Joseph of Nazareth tells us that, if human cooperation with God is excluded, then salvation, and man as such, are, quite simply, abolished.

Joseph is the strong man who in Jesus and Mary, *in* Jesus *through* Mary, becomes the new man. The Church as a people of the redeemed begins in some way with him, with his justice. He is the first "just man," the prototype of the new people, of the people with a "new heart" (Ezek. 36:26), whose original characteristic is birth not in the flesh but in the Spirit (see John 3:5–6).

We have now arrived, nearly as a glorious finale, at St. Joseph as guardian of the Church. The treasurer of God receives, as a gift from the Son through Mary, his spouse, the bulwark of faith and of grace, the flawless sanctity of the Church, Body of Christ and Bride of the Lamb. Joseph has the Church in his hands: the Head, Christ, and the members already united in one another in the womb of Mary, the Woman of Calvary, and already present in her as in the most perfect realization. Joseph possesses Jesus and Mary; in the two of them, he is reborn as the son of God.

Joseph has a primacy among the redeemed—after Mary's unique redemption, the Immaculate Conception—in the order of subjective Redemption. At the same time, his con-salvific work is inserted into the very effectuating of the Redemption. He collaborates with Jesus and with Mary and, through his co-redemptive collaboration, completes in his flesh the sufferings of Christ for the good of the whole Church (see Col. 1:24). Joseph is the beginning of the redeemed people; he is the model of the redeemed because he alone had the grace to support Jesus and Mary in the accomplishing of so much work: he did so by receiving everything from them, by co-immolating everything in them. Joseph offered himself, his sufferings, his whole life to Jesus by means of Mary in the very unfolding of our Redemption, that is, at the very moment of the accomplishing of the salvific work of the Son and of His mother, of the Redeemer and of the Co-redemptrix.

The spousal love of Joseph and of Mary became a salvific echo of the spousal love of the Redeemer and the Co-redemptrix. While Jesus and Mary sacrificed themselves for our salvation at each moment of their human journey, Joseph breathed in those united tremors of love and sorrow, making them vibrate in his own flesh. All the sighs of sorrowful love and loving sorrow coming from the Son and the Bride reverberated with acute accents in his heart as well. Joseph, who had said his *fiat* to God by means of Mary, now extended his obedience to the mystery, saying his *fiat* also for us. Joseph's *fiat* becomes the melodious echo of that of the Son (see Heb. 10:7) and of that of Mary (see Luke 1:38) and is prolonged in the furrows of that field which is the Church (see 1 Cor. 3:9), through which the unique salvation is given to us by the Redeemer and the Co-redemptrix.

Joseph of Nazareth becomes Co-redeemer for us all, and is a model for us all, in the Redeemer and in the Co-redemptrix. He stands in the Church as the model of redeemed men who actively collaborate in the salvation of the world. That is why he is the guardian of the Church.

He is the guardian of the mystery of the Redemption. He is the guardian of those who effectuate the Redemption: his Son and his spouse. Joseph offers his life, his person, to God in the service of the mystery of salvation. When gazing at him, men are drawn to God, having a model of authentic Christian life. Joseph opens to us the mystery of the Church in his person: his yes to God through Mary is a definitive, irrevocable gift of self, until his last breath; it is the giving of himself in the longing for the kingdom. St. Joseph throughout his life experiences this longing for the possession of that kingdom where God is, and is already beginning to be in us, uniting us to himself in Mary, so that we may be his collaborators in our own salvation and in that of others (see 2 Tim. 2:10).

Joseph, more than any other saint, more than Paul himself, can exclaim: "If we are afflicted, it is for your comfort and salvation; and if we are comforted, it is for your comfort, which you experience when you patiently endure the same sufferings that we suffer" (2 Cor. 1:6).

St. Joseph is, then, a faithful icon of the Church, the body gathered by the Father through Christ in the Spirit, a people loved, redeemed, saved. However, if we look closely, all the precious goods of Joseph, his privileged position with respect to every baptized person, come to him from Mary. It is the Virgin who gives Jesus to Joseph and, along with Jesus, every other gift: salvation and eternal life. Mary is the bridge between Joseph and Christ. She is the Mediatrix in the Mediator.

Joseph "took his wife" with him (Matt. 1:24). After this solemn moment, Joseph will take "the child and his mother" (Matt. 2:13-14, 20-21). The Child, his son, will take precedence, that Child whom Mary had placed in his arms, making him the "father" of a great mystery. And whereas in Matthew's Gospel the Magi "saw the child with Mary his mother" (Matt. 2:11), Luke is not afraid to present the father figure of Joseph in that beautiful passage: the shepherds who went to the stable in Bethlehem "found Mary and Joseph, and the babe lying in a manger" (Luke 2:16).

Through Mary we go to Jesus, and Joseph is the most authentic witness who attests to this. He, the Saint of Nazareth, so humble, now breaks his mystical silence and says to each one of us: " 'Do not fear to take Mary' with you (Matt. 1:20), as she alone leads you to Jesus, she alone gives you Jesus, the Savior." In order to summarize in some way his figure and his presence in the Church, we may say that Joseph is ultimately the model of consecration to Mary, of the sponsality of love with the Virgin of Nazareth. St. Joseph, so reserved, shy, and reluctant to make his voice heard, stands majestically in the Church as father and spouse, two dimensions lived in his filial *agape* with God. Joseph of Nazareth, the new man, the living reflection of the holy Church, hands over to us this program of Christian life· *with* Mary and *in* Mary to Christ in the Spirit to adore the Father.

Chapter 10

Joseph of Nazareth, Model of Our Workaday Life

Before delving more deeply into this mystery of Joseph in our spiritual life, as model of Marian consecration, let us take a moment to reflect on his presence in our daily working life. Joseph of Nazareth, guardian of the life of the Church, is guardian of the life of each member of this Mystical Body. It is therefore fitting to take a moment to reflect on the importance of human work, of which St. Joseph is an outstanding model, as well as its sanctification by Jesus and Mary.

Significantly, in order to counter the rise of massive anarchical laborers' protests, which demanded rights for workers (usually as a veil for materialistic ideology), Pius XII established the feast of St. Joseph the Worker on the first of May. This was declared through an address to a Catholic Association of Italian Workers in 1955. Through the same speech, Pius XII also wanted to reassure all Catholics that Mother Church has always shown concern for workers, emphasizing the dignity of work and the need for justice, which should always guide all human actions, while simultaneously condemning the exploitation of workers.

The pope wanted to rebuke above all the vicious calumny, spread by Marxists and socialists, according to which "The Church is an ally of capitalism against the workers." The true problem underlying this Marxist protest against religion, and the Catholic Faith in particular, was the materialistic vision of man and society.

Work was seen as something demeaning our human condition. The exploitation of workers, which did in fact exist, could only be remedied, according to this ideology, by restricting individual rights, such as private property, which supposedly were the cause of social inequality. Men dreamed of transforming the selfishness of a few into the general well-being of the many. They longed for a communist society where everyone would share their belongings, with neither social classes nor any differences between men—and, moreover, without the family.

The distinction between husband, wife, and children was supposedly the very reason for the original social classification, as it postulated natural hierarchical roles. Instead, these ideologues wanted an open society, without distinctions, and, above all, without God: with neither the Creator nor the Redeemer. Working to perfect oneself and to contribute to the greater good of humanity's supernatural heritage was in no way conceivable. The very reason why man supposedly suffered from social alienation was, ultimately, not simply work nor an economy based on selfishness but, rather, God and religion.

Our Lady came to Fatima in 1917. In her third apparition, on July 13, she warned humanity, through the feeble voice of three little children, that if her call to consecrate Russia to her Immaculate Heart—together with personal repentance and sacrifice—was not heeded, Russia would spread the toxic errors of materialism and communism throughout the world. Does this ring any bells today?

Can we say that Our Lady was wrong when we see around us a new empire governed only by matter, with a materialistic ideology that has become an ideal goal also in the Church? Man decides what he wants to be: whether he is male or female, human or transhuman, or perhaps post-human. Economic crises and pandemics seem to worry us the most. God Himself is replaced by new ecological interests for the new goddess "mother earth," with human pretensions "to save the planet"—concerns which have taken the place of God. We have become the god we adore.

However, the teaching of the Church is also very clear in condemning the error opposed to communism, which is economic liberalism, in which individual freedom—including the absolute freedom to be selfish—is set against the common good. Work, according to this system, is also a burden, and man is called to free himself from this burden through unbridled competition, laying the burden on the shoulders of his underlings. Work is despised, but without being eliminated, because in any case some person or some powerful group will derive profits by exploiting those who are subordinate.

It might also happen, in the not-too-distant future, that both socialism and liberalism (two sides of the same coin) become one by conceiving an updated economic environment, where men would be deprived of their private goods and property, so that each one can contribute to the common cause of a new shared economy, which is controlled, however, by the financial benefactors of this new earthly paradise. This would simply be another way to enslave man through the work of his own hands, in the name of man and of the socialist ideology.

The problem is that work is not redeemed because there is no Redemption. God is the true guardian of man and his dignity, and yet we have turned our backs on Him. In both cases, socialism and liberalism, work is an overwhelming burden and not a sweet yoke transformed by the love of Christ. Man, according to this ideology, is made for work rather than work for man, for his human and spiritual growth.

Pius XII, by inaugurating the feast of St. Joseph the Worker, wanted to tell all men that work has a dignity in itself, as it is a participation in God's care for His creation and has a special share in Christ's new creation, in the *recapitulation* of all things in His blood by His death on the Cross.

The *Catechism* teaches us, in this regard, that:

Human work proceeds directly from persons created in the image of God and called to prolong the work of creation by subduing the earth, both with and for one another. Hence work is a duty: "If anyone will not work, let him not eat." Work honors the Creator's gifts and the talents received from him. It can also be redemptive. By enduring the hardship of work in union with Jesus, the carpenter of Nazareth and the one crucified on Calvary, man collaborates in a certain fashion with the Son of God in his redemptive work. (2427)

Any kind of work is worthy of a person so long as it is a participation in the work of Redemption. Being an architect, a doctor, a workman, a farmer, or a housewife has equal dignity before God inasmuch as one works for Him and with Him. The work of being a father and a mother, raising children according to God's law and love, is worthy of a man and a woman: this is the most precious work needed today in order to make our society human again.

The fatigue and pain attached to work are effects of Original Sin. However, when man works in union with Christ and transforms his labor into an offering of love, that work, redeemed in Christ, plays a very fundamental role in the salvation of mankind.

We must be happy because our personal work, anything we do with love and for the sake of love, is redeemed, that is, is spared from being mere alienation of man or usurpation of his dignity. In Christ we are no longer subject to sin. It is sin, egoism, greed, self-sufficiency that enslave man, impoverish him, whether he is exploiting others or is exploited by others.

St. Joseph today stands out as the model of every worker. Chosen by God to be the father of His son, it is he who introduced Jesus to work and taught Him how to work. The Son of God sanctified our human endeavor with the work of His own hands. He saw Joseph working and imitated him. St. Joseph, in turn, shows us Jesus our Savior. The greatest work is the one by which we have been saved, the work of Redemption. Redeeming is equivalent to "working" by offering oneself, one's life. In this praiseworthy and unparalleled work, Our Lady and St. Joseph, the Mother Co-redemptrix and the Father Co-redeemer, played a unique part. Let us ask them for the grace to be faithful to our work and to transform the work of our hands into a means of sanctification and of salvation for us and for many.

Chapter 11

Holy Joseph,
Model of our Devotional Life

Not only is St. Joseph a model for our working life but, even more importantly, for our devotional life. St. Peter Julian Eymard says that "When God wants to raise a soul to greater heights, he unites this soul to St. Joseph, inspiring a great love for the good saint." How can we measure the great love of the saints for our Joseph of Nazareth, unparalleled for his lofty mission and holiness? And couldn't we, too, do likewise?

We read about many examples of devotion to this great saint in the lives of the saints, as Fr. Stefano M. Manelli tells us in his precious *Mese di San Giuseppe.*

St. Margaret of Cortona (1247–1297), out of devotion, used to recite one hundred *Pater Nosters* in honor of St. Joseph as the foster father of the Savior and then another hundred for the obedience of Jesus toward him.

St. Pio of Pietrelcina (1887–1968) was also known for his great love for St. Joseph. He loved to recite every day, in addition to many Rosaries, the Chaplet of the Sacred Heart, which ended with the invocation: "St. Joseph, friend of the Sacred Heart of Jesus, pray for us."

However, according to Padre Pio, the attribute of "friend" with which St. Joseph was qualified was inadequate compared to the greatness of the saint. And he pointed this out to the members of his religious community whom he gathered together in prayer. One day, his confreres asked Padre Pio how, according to him, St. Joseph ought to be addressed. And this was his response:

"According to me?... He must be addressed according to Sacred Scripture ... and according to Sacred Scripture, St. Joseph is the foster father of Jesus, he is the one who acted as father towards Jesus." And he immediately added the quotation from another scriptural passage, in which the Virgin Mary refers to Joseph as a father: "your father and I have been looking for you anxiously" (Luke 2:48). Joseph is precisely the foster father, Padre Pio forcefully affirmed.[25]

After this conversation, the friars changed the invocation to St. Joseph and began to say: "St. Joseph, foster father of the Sacred Heart of Jesus, pray for us." When Padre Pio heard this, he was moved.

Another great devotee of St. Joseph was Bl. Bartolo Longo. Here is a sampling of his sentiments toward St. Joseph:

Who could possibly tell us, O most blessed Joseph, what was the sweetness of your thoughts, the humility of your spirit when Jesus called you His father and you called Him *my dear son?*... With what heavenly fervour your soul must have been filled when you took Jesus for a walk, when you served him or carried him in your arms, He who was your all?... And that divine Child gave you back a thousand kisses, caressed you with His little hands, smiled at you

---

[25] Manelli, *Il mese di San Giuseppe*, 27–28, our translation.

lovingly.... What were your thoughts when you taught Him how to walk, He who, by one great leap, had come down from Heaven to earth to visit men? What was the first word you taught the substantial and eternal Word to pronounce?[26]

This is just a brief sampling of the mellifluous sentiments that Bl. Bartolo Longo cultivated in his assiduous prayers to the one who, after Mary, is a giant of holiness and to whom he invited everyone to give their hearts. We, too, should imitate the saints in their love for St. Joseph.

Better yet, we should imitate Jesus who was obedient to St. Joseph and to His mother. Luke's text tells us that Jesus, having returned to Nazareth after having been found in the temple, "Erat subditus illis," he "was obedient to them" (Luke 2:51). This is how St. Ambrose, in his *Exposition of the Holy Gospel according to St. Luke* (8:74), comments on these words:

> Christ honoured Joseph and Mary, not because it was a debt owed them by nature (*naturae debito*), but because it was a duty he owed to love (*pietatis officio*). He also honoured God His Father as no other person has ever been able to honour Him. And He was obedient even to death. So, you, too, must honour your parents.

Dear reader, may you, too, honor the great St. Joseph.

We began by talking about the meaning of the name "Joseph," and we quoted the formula of blessing with which Jacob blesses Joseph (Gen. 49:25–26). Now, as we near our conclusion, we wish to present another blessing addressed to the ancient Joseph.

---

[26] Ibid., 29, our translation.

Before dying, Moses saw from afar the Land that the Lord had promised him but into which he could not enter because of his infidelity at the waters of Meribath-kadesh, and he blessed the Israelites (Deut. 32:48–33:1). To Joseph he addressed this blessing:

> Blessed by the LORD be his land,
>> with the choicest gifts of heaven above,
>> and of the deep that couches beneath,
> with the choicest fruits of the sun,
>> and the rich yield of the months,
> with the finest produce of the ancient mountains,
>> and the abundance of the everlasting hills,
> with the best gifts of the earth and its fulness,
>> and the favor of him that dwelt in the bush.
> Let these come upon the head of Joseph,
>> and upon the crown of the head of him that is
>>> prince among his brothers.
> His firstling bull has majesty,
>> and his horns are the horns of a wild ox;
> with them he shall push the peoples,
>> all of them, to the ends of the earth;
> such are the ten thousands of Ephraim,
>> and such are the thousands of Manasseh.
>> (Deut. 33:13–17)

The dew is a biblical symbol that portrays St. Joseph quite well, his delicate descent upon the earth, covering it with a layer that preserves the harvest and irrigates it, just as the dew does at dawn. The dew depicts his silence, his mystery, which cloaked the "virgin earth," his spouse, and thus allowed the most beautiful fruit, Jesus, to blossom forth.

The silence of the night when the dew falls is an image of the whole life of our St. Joseph. With his loving attentiveness, and in a delicate, acquiescent, and docile way, he enveloped the mysteries of God. He guarded them with the mantle of his prayerful, ever-present, steadfast love. Shouldn't we strive to be a bit like him?

There is an episode from the life of St. Bernardine of Siena in which, as he was preaching one day in Padua before a large audience, being all intent on proclaiming the greatness of St. Joseph, and in particular his assumption into heaven in body and soul, there was seen a golden Cross glowing over his head, which appeared to miraculously approve of what Bernardine was teaching. And so, the prayer that this saint composed in honor of the foster father of Jesus and the spouse of Mary should be dear to us. Here it is in the original with our translation:

> Memento nostri, Beate Joseph, et tuae orationis suffragio apud tuum Putativum Filium intercedes: sed, et Beatis-simam Virginem, Sponsam tuam nobis propitiam redde, quae Mater est eius, qui Patre, et Spiritu Sancto vivit, et regnat per infinita saecula saeculorum.

> Remember us, O Blessed Joseph, and through your prayers … intercede with your foster Son; render the Most Blessed Virgin propitious to us, she who is your Spouse, the Mother of the One who, with the Father and the Holy Spirit, lives and reigns for ever and ever.[27]

Let us often recite this prayer to our great craftsman, who, in the words of St. Jacob of Sarug, is the minister of the Craftsman of

---

[27] Giuseppe Antonio Patrignani, S.J., *Il devoto di San Giuseppe* (Venice, 1724), 478–479.

the world, or who, in the words of St. Ambrose, is a *type* of the Father, Craftsman of all that exist.

Let us pray to this virgin spouse of Mary ever virgin, Guardian of heavenly treasures, Propitiatory of the Ark of God, so that he may deign to grant our most important supplication: to be found one day with him in Heaven, beside his Son and his spouse, members of the holy Family of God, crystal-clear mirror of the heavenly Trinity, of which the Church on earth is an anticipation and a pathway.

The Prototype of Marian Consecration

Our theological and spiritual reflections thus lead us to prayer and devotion, and before ending with some prayers, both ancient and new, to our beloved saint, let us reflect on the role of St. Joseph in leading us, in an exemplary way, to the truest and deepest Marian devotion. We can discover, in his "taking Mary with him," a doctrine that uniquely preludes his consecration to Mary and therefore becomes the paradigm of every consecration to her.

Let us recall the concept of "taking his spouse with him," by emphasizing the mystery of the union of St. Joseph with the Blessed Virgin Mary. As we have seen, it is in this union that we find the source of all the graces of the Josephine mystery, and it is through this union that the Saint of Nazareth is introduced by the New Testament and is known in the Church. Having looked carefully at his life, we have seen that everything happens through Mary. Joseph begins to be known as Mary's spouse (see Matt. 1:16) and, precisely because of this spousal relationship, he is introduced into the mystery of Christ, becoming His foster father. All comes to Joseph *through* Mary.

Let us ponder a moment on the Gospel of Matthew (1:18–19), where Joseph of Nazareth is presented first of all as Mary's spouse and then as a "just man":

> Now the birth of Jesus Christ took place in this way. When his mother Mary had been betrothed to Joseph, before they came together she was found to be with child of the Holy Spirit; and her husband Joseph, being a just man and unwilling to put her to shame, resolved to send her away quietly.

Thanks to this passage, we have understood that Mary and Joseph were already married when the Virgin miraculously became pregnant with her son Jesus. By saying "betrothed," the Gospel highlights the Hebrew custom of celebrating marriage in two moments: the legal union, as a true marriage with all civil and religious effects, and cohabitation that could take place even a year after the promise of marriage. The Gospel of Luke also reports that Joseph was already united to Mary by a marriage covenant. In fact, the angel was sent "to a virgin betrothed to a man whose name was Joseph, of the house of David" (1:27).

From this blessed spousal union with Mary, the relationship of St. Joseph with Jesus also takes shape. The holy carpenter comes into personal contact with Jesus through Our Lady when it is he who gives the name "Jesus" to Mary's son (Matt. 1:21). Even at the moment of adoration of the shepherds, who arrived in haste to see the sign of God, Joseph is between Mary and Jesus: "They went with haste, and found Mary and Joseph, and the babe lying in a manger," the Gospel tells us (Luke 2:16), as if to say that the Christian path that leads to discovering fully who that Child is goes *from Mary to Jesus.*

At the moment of Jesus' finding in the temple, Joseph is once again between Mary and Jesus. The Virgin emphasizes this position of her beloved spouse in the mystery of the Holy Family when she lovingly points out to her son, with a tone of regret: "Your father and I have been looking for you anxiously" (Luke 2:48). Through his espousal with Mary, Joseph embraces Jesus and holds Him in his arms. He is therefore the most perfect icon of consecration to Mary, of the classic adage: *ad Jesum per Mariam*: to Jesus through Mary.

Let us return once again to the unique and virginal marriage of St. Joseph with Our Lady, as it is the true key to understanding the figure of the Carpenter of Nazareth as the first *type* or exemplary model of Marian consecration.

This holy marriage was undoubtedly extraordinary. In considering this mystery, we must transcend its natural meaning and aim directly at the depth of its spiritual aspect. In fact, everything points in favor of a special and entirely spiritual union. In the account of St. Matthew (1:18–19) just quoted, about the fact that Joseph was already espoused to Mary although they did not yet live together, we can discover something more by virtue of an anagogical interpretation of the text. That is, although Joseph was already legally united in matrimony to Mary, he was not yet fully united to her.

We could interpret this in the sense of his not yet being *consecrated* to her, since their cohabitation would have been, by mutual agreement, virginal and chaste. This Josephite marriage should be considered in the light of two superior moments: the initial marital union and its consummation, to be understood as signifying consecration to Mary, a full gift of himself to the Virgin.

The consummation of marriage thus acquires a new spiritual meaning, foretelling Jesus' mystical marriage with the Church on the Cross. Just as for Jesus Crucified, the gift of self to the Spouse is "consummated" in His love "to the end" (John 13:1), a total love unto death, so it is for St. Joseph. His total love for Mary is consummated in the sacrifice of himself unto death to be one with Mary, in order to participate in the Redemption of Christ. This consecration to Mary happens after the angel's revelation, when Joseph has full knowledge of who Mary is and who the Son is whom she is carrying in her womb. Now Joseph is ready to take Mary into his life and, through her, to take care of Jesus.

We can contemplate all this in the light of the account of Matthew's Gospel (1:20–24), in which we read:

> But as he considered this, behold, an angel of the Lord appeared to him in a dream, saying, "Joseph, son of David, do not fear to take Mary your wife, for that which is conceived in her is of the Holy Spirit; she will bear a son, and you shall call his name Jesus, for he will save his people from their sins." All this took place to fulfil what the Lord had spoken by the prophet:
>
> > "Behold, a virgin shall conceive and bear a son,
> >   and his name shall be called Emmanuel"
>
> (which means, God with us). When Joseph woke from sleep, he did as the angel of the Lord commanded him; he took his wife.

We should focus above all on the last sentence of this pericope, which in the original Greek reads as follows: "Kai parélaben tèn gunaîka autou" ("He took his spouse with him" [or more literally his "woman"]). The verb *para-lambano*, "to take," generally has two meanings: (1) to take with oneself, to unite to oneself, or (2) to receive that which is transmitted.

Let us recall that this verb is the same one that we find in the Gospel of John (19:27), which designates the act of taking/receiving Mary in one's life on the part of the beloved disciple:

"And from that hour the disciple took her to his own home" (the original says: "Élaben o mathetès autèn eis ta ídia," "He took her among his things, his most cherished ones"). John welcomed Mary, the Woman, whom Jesus now designates as his mother. As we have already seen, the mother of Jesus becomes the mother of John, insofar as she is the New Eve beside the New Adam. Mary, as the Woman, the New Eve, is associated with Christ the Redeemer, as His Co-redemptrix.

Therefore, we can easily conclude that Joseph, before any other, *from that hour took* Mary with him, that is, from the hour in which he was instructed by the angel, by means of the Holy Spirit, the mystery of Mary and the Child in her womb. Joseph, like John, but well before him, took Mary with him—she who begets the children of God. Generated by her to the life of grace and united to her, he will thereafter entrust her to John and, through John, to all of us. Joseph's act of welcoming Mary therefore anticipates, in a certain manner, Our Lord's words on the Cross to the beloved disciple concerning His Mother. Joseph is thus the prototype of the beloved disciple.

From the moment of his full and perfect union with Mary, Joseph entrusted himself entirely to her, so that through her, he could enter into the mystery of Christ and participate actively in the work of the Redemption. Therefore, as John will do at Calvary, welcoming Mary, Joseph has already done, and even more perfectly, at the announcement of the angel.

This link between Joseph and John, consisting for each in taking Mary with him, of welcoming her, is established by St. John Chrysostom in his commentary on the Gospel of Matthew. The angel reassures Joseph and entrusts him with the custody of Mary. He will have to keep her with him: it is God Himself who gives her to him:

He commits her to you, not for the ordinary usage of marriage, but only that she may dwell with you; and by my voice does He commit her to you. Just as Christ Himself hereafter will commit her to His disciple, so even now unto Joseph does He commit her (*Ioseph traditur*). (*In Matthaeum*, 4, 6)

Later in his homily Chrysostom tackles the tempting tendency to doubt the virginity of St. Joseph, and he returns to the theme of Mary's entrustment to Joseph, as thereafter to John at the foot of the Cross:

For if he had known her (*uxoris loco*), and lived with her as his wife, and had had children with her as some have dared to suggest, how is it that our Lord from the Cross commits her to His disciple, as if she were unprotected and had no one to care for her, and commands him to take her to his own home? How is it then, some may enquire, that in the Gospel, James, John and some others are called His brethren? They were called the brethren of Jesus in the same way that Joseph was called the husband of Mary (*Ibid.*, 5, 3).

One last point must be clarified in order to present a complete picture of the marriage of St. Joseph with Mary as a consecration to her. The fact that the marriage was virginal is of great importance. This proves that Joseph's complete surrender of himself to Mary, during the second phase of the wedding, must be understood as the spiritual consummation of that union.

The Gospel, emphasizing the way in which Joseph welcomes Mary into his life, also says: "But knew her not until she had borne a son; and he called his name Jesus" (Matt. 1:25). This is certainly the correct translation of the original text which, nonetheless, presents the particle *until* (*éos*). The preposition *until*, however, does not mean that after Jesus' birth, Mary and Joseph had normal marital relations.

In fact, there are several biblical examples in which *until* never implies a later change. We can recall, among many, for example, the words of the messianic Psalm (110:1): "The Lord says to my lord: 'Sit at my right hand, till I make your enemies your footstool.'" Obviously, Christ does not reign at the right hand of the Father only until His enemies are defeated. Even when Jesus promised His apostles to remain with them "to the close of the age" (Matt. 28:20), He did not want to imply that He would be with them only until the Parousia.

On the contrary. With the temporal preposition *until*, the evangelist wishes to say that Joseph and Mary, unlike an ordinary Jewish couple, did not consummate their marriage on their wedding night. This was because Mary had taken a vow of virginity, as is clearly evident from her reply to the angel: "I have no husband" (Luke 1:34). This was not unknown to Jewish tradition but was a vow of abstinence according to the book of Numbers (chap. 30) which Joseph had accepted and then endorsed.

The conclusion we can draw from this final reflection is that Joseph paves the way for us to be totally devoted to Mary. This great Patriarch is our model of consecration to Mary. Just as St. Joseph received Mary into his life, so likewise we must welcome her into our life. This receiving of Mary on the part of St. Joseph meant, first of all, that he was to share his whole life with Mary: his thoughts, his will, his belongings, in order to please Jesus and to do God's will.

Joseph was virginally obedient to Mary in order to be conformed to Jesus' obedience to the Father. He loved Mary with all his chaste heart so as to remain ever vigilant in his ministry as guardian of Christ and servant of the Redemption. He remained devoutly in the presence of Mary so as to always be in the presence of Jesus. Knowing who Mary is meant, for Joseph, knowing who God is, knowing where He dwells.

Our own consecration to Mary, which St. Joseph was the first to make, and in a most perfect way, should then aim at obtaining *in primis* that chaste Josephine disposition of heart. To the extent that we love Our Lady with a pure heart, with the pure heart of St. Joseph, in response, she will welcome us under her mantle of purity and make us her spouses of love. In this way, through this espousal with Mary, we will be safe from all the snares of impurity and impiety present in the world. May St. Joseph be even better known as the Patriarch of love *for Jesus through Mary* and in his role as mystical spouse of the Blessed Virgin. To this we say: *Amen!*

Chapter 12

Mighty Intercessor

Just as Joseph leads us to Jesus through Mary, so likewise we can well imagine how joy-filled Our Lady and Our Lord must be to see souls render to Holy Joseph the *protodulia* due to him. For this reason, it is highly fitting to conclude our theological investigation and spiritual reflections on St. Joseph by offering a sampling of prayers addressed to this great saint, so that the reader may grow in veneration of this saint through prayer.

The deepened knowledge and understanding we acquire must lead us to greater devotion, by praying with love and devotion to a saint whose mystery we have come to know more profoundly. By that law dear to Christianity of the interweaving of *lex credendi* and *lex orandi*, by praying, the doctrine possessed by the intellect shines in a clearer light and is welcomed more easily by the will fortified by grace. Our prayer must be grounded in a right understanding of the mysteries of the Faith, and our deepened understanding must lead us to prayer, to a deepened devotion and more fervent piety.

Firstly, the reader will find two beautiful prayers to St. Joseph which were composed by two great Marian, and therefore Josephine, saints: St. Louis-Marie Grignion de Montfort and St. John Eudes. Then, these prayers are followed by a new Litany in Praise of St. Joseph which we have composed and offer to our readers to enhance their Josephine piety. Finally, there is the Chaplet of the Seven Sorrows and the Seven Joys of St. Joseph, supplemented by meditations which we likewise offer to our readers in order to nourish their meditation and increase their devotion to our beloved saint.

Josephine Prayers by Two Great Marian Saints

Hail Joseph
by St. Louis-Marie Grignion de Montfort[28]

Hail Joseph the just, Wisdom is with you; blessed are you among all men and blessed is Jesus, the fruit of Mary, your faithful spouse. Holy Joseph, worthy foster-father of Jesus Christ, pray for us sinners and obtain divine Wisdom for us from God, now and at the hour of our death. *Amen.*

Praises of St. Joseph
by St. John Eudes[29]

Hail Joseph, image of God the Father.
Hail Joseph, father of God the Son.
Hail Joseph, temple of the Holy Spirit.
Hail Joseph, beloved of the Most Holy Trinity.
Hail Joseph, most faithful coadjutor of the great counsel.

---

[28] St. Louis-Marie Grignion de Montfort, *Methods of Reciting the Rosary*, no. 12.

[29] Quoted in Donald H. Calloway, M.I.C., *Consecration to St. Joseph: The Wonders of Our Spiritual Father* (Stockbridge: Marian Press, 2020), 244.

Hail Joseph, most worthy spouse of the Virgin Mary.
Hail Joseph, father of all the faithful.
Hail Joseph, guardian of all those who have embraced
    holy virginity.
Hail Joseph, faithful observer of holy silence.
Hail Joseph, lover of holy poverty.
Hail Joseph, model of meekness and patience.
Hail Joseph, mirror of humility and obedience.
Blessed art thou above all men.
Blessed thine eyes, which have seen the things which
    thou hast seen.
Blessed thine ears, which have heard the things which
    thou hast heard.
Blessed thy hands, which have touched and handled
    the Incarnate Word.
Blessed thine arms, which have borne Him who bears
    all things.
Blessed thy bosom, on which the Son of God fondly
    rested.
Blessed thy heart, inflamed with burning love.
Blessed be the Eternal Father, who chose thee.
Blessed be the Son, who loved thee.
Blessed be the Holy Spirit, who sanctified thee.
Blessed be Mary, thy spouse, who cherished thee as
    her spouse and brother.
Blessed be the angel who served thee as a guardian,
And blessed forever be all who love and bless thee.
Amen.

A New Litany of Praise for St. Joseph

We can never say enough about St. Joseph, as we made clear at the very beginning of this volume. The *protodulia* due to him, which is second only to the *hyperdulia* due to the Blessed Virgin Mary, encourages us to conceive new songs of praise in honor of St. Joseph, after exploring new horizons of the Josephine mystery, as we have attempted to do in this study.

Thus was born this new litany to St. Joseph, which we offer to the reader as a prayer of devotion and praise to our Patriarch. Far from seeking to replace the official litanies approved by the Church, we simply wish to express the pious desire to synthesize the preceding chapters and transpose their substance into a Josephine hymn.

Before presenting our new litany, let us say a word of the official litanies in honor of St. Joseph, which were approved by the Apostolic See in 1909 (see *Acta Apostolicae Sedis* 1 [1909]: 290–292). Recently, in light of the Year of Joseph instituted by Pope Francis and his Apostolic Letter *Patris corde* (December 8, 2020), these litanies have been updated to include seven new invocations, taken from the speeches of recent popes, namely: *Custos Redemptoris* (see John Paul II, Apostolic Exhortation *Redemptoris custos*); *Serve Christi* (see Paul VI, Homily of March 19 , 1966, quoted in *Redemptoris custos*, no. 8 and *Patris corde*, no. 1); *Minister salutis* (St. John Chrysostom, quoted in *Redemptoris custos*, no. 8); *Fulcimen in difficultatibus* (see *Patris corde*, prologue); and *Patrone exsulum, afflictorum, pauperum* (see *Patris corde*, no. 5). See the Letter to the Presidents of the Bishops' Conferences on the New Invocations in the Litanies in Honor of St. Joseph, May 1, 2021.

Let us now move on to the new litany which we have composed in honor of St. Joseph, a prayerful contribution that desires to humbly hide behind the official litanies, as an echo capable of resonating in the mind and heart of the reader, inviting him to praise St. Joseph once again, saying:

Lord, *have mercy on us.*
Christ, *have mercy on us.*
Lord, *have mercy on us.*
Christ, *hear us.*
Christ, *graciously hear us.*
God the Father of Heaven, *have mercy on us.*
God the Son, Redeemer of the World, *have mercy on us.*
God the Holy Spirit, *have mercy on us.*
Holy Trinity, one God, *have mercy on us.*
Holy Mary, *pray for us.*
St. Joseph, *pray for us.*
Spouse of the Blessed Virgin Mary, *pray for us.*
Prototype of consecration to Mary, *pray for us.*
First John given to Mary, *pray for us.*
Beloved disciple of the Most High, *pray for us.*
Father of the divine Savior, *pray for us.*
Guardian of divine treasures, *pray for us.*
Impregnable fortress, *pray for us.*
Protector and guardian of Mary's virginity, *pray for us.*
Virginal Spouse of the Queen of Virgins, *pray for us.*
Co-redeemer in the Co-redemptrix, *pray for us.*
Unique cooperator in our salvation, *pray for us.*
Model of participation in Christ's priesthood, *pray for us.*
Admirable Father, *pray for us.*
Earthly image of divine paternity, *pray for us.*

Mirror of justice and holiness, *pray for us.*
Guardian of silence, *pray for us.*
Supreme contemplator of the divine mysteries, *pray for us.*
Faithful servant of the Lord, *pray for us.*
Defender of Mother Church, *pray for us.*
Faithful guardian of the holy doctrine, *pray for us.*
Model of faith, hope, and charity, *pray for us.*
Figure of Christ the Bridegroom of the Church, *pray for us.*
Fulfillment of the figures of the patriarchs, *pray for us.*
New Abraham, *pray for us.*
True Noah, *pray for us.*
New Moses, *pray for us.*
True Joseph of Egypt, *pray for us.*
Heavenly dew, *pray for us.*
Perfume of all virtues, *pray for us.*
Apostle before the apostles and more than the apostles,
    pray for us.
Model of martyrs, *pray for us.*
Precursor of the Lord, *pray for us.*
Mirror of virgins, *pray for us.*
Father of the poor, *pray for us.*
Educator of the Most High, *pray for us.*
Worker for God, *pray for us.*
Comforter of the dying, *pray for us.*
Model of sacrifice, *pray for us.*
Most humble Joseph, *pray for us.*
Lover of discretion, *pray for us.*
Fullness of divine holiness, *pray for us.*
Father in love with every Christian, *pray for us.*
Infallible guide to Christ through Mary, *pray for us.*
Shadow of divine providence, *pray for us.*

Supreme Adorer of the Father, *pray for us.*
Illustrious doctor of the faith, *pray for us.*
Lover of purity, *pray for us.*
Chosen vessel, *pray for us.*
Most Holy Joseph, *pray for us.*

> V. *Pray for us, O most faithful Guardian of the divine mysteries.*
>
> R. *That we may be made worthy of the promises of Jesus Christ, your son.*

Let us pray: O Father, who in St. Joseph offered your Church an illustrious and incomparable model of Christian perfection, grant that by imitating the example of Christ your Son, we, too, may place ourselves under his paternal patronage, so that by becoming one with Mary, his spouse, we may receive the gift of the Holy Spirit and with him attain eternal bliss. Through Jesus Christ our Lord. *Amen.*

The Seven Joys and Sorrows
of St. Joseph Chaplet

In order to prepare ourselves to meditate on the sorrowful and joyful mysteries of Joseph, let us take a moment to contemplate this holy image.

As is the case with the enamel plaque we have already briefly pored over, this stained-glass window likewise presents a rare rendering of the Gospel scene of the circumcision of Jesus, in that it is Joseph who is depicted as accomplishing the holy rite. However, the vibrancy of the colors and the luminosity inherent to the stained glass window give to this artwork a joyful note as compared to the enamel plaque, which invites the viewer to consider more the sorrowful aspect of the mystery.

Indeed, as we will see, when we meditate on the sorrows intermingled with the joys of Joseph, this mystery of the circumcision and the naming of Jesus is twofold, both sorrowful, in the shedding of the first drop of Precious Blood, and joyful, in the knowledge that supernatural life is being given back to souls. So let us now imagine ourselves in the oratory where this image can be admired and gaze upon it for a moment:

As Joseph is accomplishing the rite of circumcision, with faith and obedience to the angel, Our luminous Lady, crowned with a star-filled halo, robed in the white of her purity and the blue of her heavenly regality, is suffused with the heavenly light shining down from the angel holding the banner with the name of Jesus inscribed on it. She gazes with hope-filled eyes at the angelic minister of God's providence, who is robed in the green of joy. Like Joseph, she knows perfectly the prophecies of the Old Testament, promising a Savior who will save mankind from sin. The joy that fills her heart and radiates from all her being is so ineffable that no words can do justice to this bliss, no word except one: *Jesus!*

Joseph, meanwhile, is intent on accomplishing the sacred rite with a priestly reverence he alone can summon from his holy heart. Though his eyes are lowered and do not contemplate the banner inscribed with the name that means salvation, his chaste heart is filled with an inner joy, a true joy that does not express itself outwardly in immodest exuberance but is all the more profound that it is soberly enshrined within his heart and enveloped in a veil of reverent discretion.

With humility, he accomplishes the great mission confided to him, that of giving the name "Jesus" to the Child, a name he imposes on Him during this rite. Joseph utters the name "Jesus," which signifies who the Child is in His very being: "God is salvation." Joseph, by accomplishing this act, announces and inaugurates the great work of Redemption, as well as of his own co-redemption.

The glory of Holy Joseph shines forth at this moment, not outwardly, but inwardly, especially within the Immaculate Heart of his Spouse, who is fully one with him in this sacred mission. He humbly kneels down before the Mother and the Child, both of whom radiate the celestial luminosity, whereas he himself is robed in the gold of glory almost entirely covered over with the purple of sacrifice.

This purple in which Joseph is draped highlights his unique priesthood as it manifests itself in this mystery, a priesthood which, though discreet, is sublime, its greatness veiled in humility. It is the priesthood of Joseph's co-redemption, of his collaboration with Jesus, through Mary, in the salvation of the human race. His sorrow is deep when hearing the tiny babe utter His first cries of pain, reminding him of the prophecy of the Suffering Servant, and making Isaiah's phrase resonate in his mind: "When he makes himself an offering for sin, he shall see his offspring, he shall prolong his days" (Isa. 53:10). Pondering these words as he gazes silently at the Divine Child and His Blessed Mother, his oneness of will and love with both of them becomes more perfect, thus transforming his sorrow into sheer bliss.

Finally, to bring our Josephine journey to a fruitful close, we offer our readership the Chaplet of the Seven Sorrows and the Seven Joys of St. Joseph, accompanied by meditations that we have composed so as to invite our readers to meditate lengthily and lovingly on the holy mysteries of the life of our beloved saint.

Our meditations wish to highlight the golden thread that binds all the salvific moments of Joseph's participation in the mystery of our salvation, namely, his sacrificial obedience, his will to offer himself with Jesus and for Jesus in all His mysteries in which he was a privileged participant.

This chaplet is comprised of seven sorrows that the piety of the faithful has long perceived in the life of the most august St. Joseph, to which were later added the seven joys, which are intertwined with the sorrows: the sorrows become joys, and the joys are the fruit of the sorrows experienced and offered.

This devotion has a Franciscan origin and dates back to the Capuchin Br. John da Fano († 1539). However, St. John Chrysostom (ca. 345–407), in his *Commentary on the Gospel of Matthew* (8:3), had already noted that the Lord took care in His goodness to mingle sweet consolations with the hardships of the holy Nurturer of Jesus. "Laboribus dulcia miscuit," "To the toils (God) mingled sweet things": this encapsulates, concisely but completely, the whole program of action and of co-redemption in Joseph's life.

Let us now conclude our Josephine journey by first contemplating a beautiful image which illustrates the most profound mystery of this chaplet, in which Joseph, as father, exercises his co-redemptive mission in a manner which is proper to him; then, by dwelling in meditation on each of Joseph's sorrows mingled with joy, remaining at the side of our beloved saint amid these co-redemptive mysteries of his life.

The Chaplet of the Seven Sorrows and the Seven Joys of St. Joseph

My God, I offer Thee this chaplet in honor of the seven sorrows and seven joys of St. Joseph, in union with the Sacred Heart of Jesus, the Immaculate Heart of Mary, and the Purest Heart of Joseph, for Thy greater glory, for my conversion and that of all men to thy beloved Son, Jesus Christ, our unique Redeemer, in union with the Holy Spirit, forever and ever. Amen.

O My God, I am heartily sorry for having offended Thee, and I detest all my sins because of Thy just punishments but, most of all, because they offend Thee, my God, who art all-good and deserving of all my love. Amen.

First Sorrow: The Inner Turmoil of St. Joseph
Her husband Joseph, being a just man and unwilling to put her to shame, resolved to send her away quietly. (Matt. 1:19)

First Joy: The Arrival of the Angel Who Comforts Joseph
But as he considered this, behold, an angel of the Lord appeared to him in a dream, saying, "Joseph, son of David, do not fear to take Mary your wife, for that which is conceived in her is of the Holy Spirit." (Matt. 1:20)

Grace of the Mystery: the virtue of purity

Meditation on Joseph's inner turmoil when he discovers that Mary is pregnant:

Mary is inhabited by God, but he does not know this. This is perhaps the most profound sorrow of Joseph's most pure heart. He does not know what is hidden in the secret of the womb of his beloved spouse, whom he believes to be most holy and whom he knows to have taken, as he himself has done, a vow of virginity. He seems to be saying to God in the secret of his heart: "How did this happen, since neither have I known my spouse nor does she want to know man even in the slightest?" He does not know. He cannot judge. Mary is pregnant, but he is not the father of that child. To repudiate his spouse would be an outrage to her holiness, to remain with her would be contrary to his justice. What to do? Finally, while his sorrowful heart was pondering all possible solutions, in order not to violate either truth or charity, an angel arrives and comforts him. So his heart rejoices. Joseph understands. He needs nothing else in order to accept God's will. He takes his spouse and obeys. A man of faith and prayer, he is always open to God's will. This is the first offering: his sacrificial obedience, entrusting all judgment to God, lived in the silence of his heart.

Pater Noster, Seven Ave Marias, Gloria Patri

Second Sorrow: Joseph's Grief at Seeing Jesus Born in Poverty
And she gave birth to her first-born son and wrapped him in swaddling cloths, and laid him in a manger, because there was no place for them in the inn. (Luke 2:7)

Second Joy: The Angelic Hymn at the Birth of Christ
And an angel of the Lord appeared to them, and the glory of the Lord shone around them, and they were filled with fear. And the angel said to them, "Be not afraid; for behold, I bring you good news of a great joy which will come to all the people; for to you is born this day in the city of David a Savior, who is Christ the Lord." (Luke 2:10–11)

Grace of the Mystery: the virtue of religion

Meditation on the pain Joseph felt in his heart upon seeing his son in the midst of so much poverty at His birth:

How St. Joseph must have suffered during the long search in order to find a hospitable place for the birth of Jesus, in a chaotic Bethlehem overflowing with people who had come there for the census. The inns were all full. And we can imagine that the homes of his distant relatives were as well. There was no room for Jesus in a makeshift house or hotel. Joseph feels regret. A place had to be found because Mary, his spouse, was about to give birth. Where to stay? After a frantic search, the Holy Family finally arrived in a hospitable place, far from all the commotion: a cave that also served as a stable. However, it was a place of extreme poverty, familiar only to the shepherds who were the first to rush there and to feel at home. What pain our Joseph must have suffered to see his Son, the King of kings, with the Most Holy Virgin, illustrious Queen, camped out in a cave. Not a soft bed but a manger was the cradle of that divine Babe. The love of Joseph's heart watched over Jesus, warmed Him with his tenderness, and already protected Him with his staff. Joseph, the good shepherd, thus introduced Jesus, the Good Shepherd, into the world. But a heavenly sign gladdened the afflicted heart of the most chaste Joseph: the joyous song of the angels who exulted and said: "Glory to God in the highest, and on earth among men with whom he is pleased!" (Luke 2:14). And so, our Joseph was ravished by Heaven with that song. His sorrow was tinged with pure joy.

Pater Noster, Seven Ave Marias, Gloria Patri

Third Sorrow: The Circumcision of Jesus
> And at the end of eight days, when he was circumcised,
> he was called Jesus, the name given by the angel before he
> was conceived in the womb. (Luke 2:21)

Third Joy: Joseph Rejoices in the Sacrifice of Salvation for All
> For from the rising of the sun to its setting my name is
> great among the nations, and in every place incense is
> offered to my name, and a pure offering; for my name
> is great among the nations, says the LORD of hosts. (Mal.
> 1:11)

Grace of the Mystery: the virtue of obedience

Meditation on the circumcision of Jesus with the shedding of the first salvific blood:

As a father, Joseph was required to make that incision himself in the flesh of the divine Babe. He did so with faith and obedience to the angel, who had told him that he would be the one to give the name "Jesus" to the child during this rite. Jesus signifies "God is salvation," and Joseph, through this priestly act, is preparing to cooperate with his son so that His first drop of blood shed may already be the blood of the Redemption. Joseph collects that blood and thus, with love and adoration, raises the first cup of salvation to Heaven (see Ps. 116:13). He may rightly say: "This is the blood of Jesus my Son, offered in expiation for all sins." At this moment, the unique priesthood of St. Joseph shines forth, a priesthood which is not sacramental but of a higher order, inferior only to that of the Most Holy Virgin. It is the priesthood of Joseph's co-redemption, of his collaboration with Jesus, through Mary, in the salvation of the human race. What sorrow he felt in seeing the tiny Babe utter His first cries of pain! It was a suffering that Joseph already sought to share to the fullest extent while meditating upon the prophecy of the suffering Servant of YHWH (see Isa. 52:13–15; 53:1–12). Isaiah's phrase kept recurring to his mind: "Yet it was the will of the Lord to bruise him; he has put him to grief; when he makes himself an offering for sin, he shall see his offspring, he shall prolong his days" (Isa. 53:10). Jesus' suffering was entirely enclosed within his fatherly heart. He would have liked to take it all upon himself, if he had been able. In silence he gazed at that sweet Child and became more and more one with Him in will and in love. But then this sorrow was transformed into joy. Sorrow is not for sorrow's sake but for love's sake. Jesus' suffering, His blood, would suffice to save everyone, even if not everyone would welcome Him. The Church would be founded precisely on this blood. From one place to another on earth, a sacrifice of salvation would be offered (see Mal. 1:11). From this sorrow a greater love was born.

Pater Noster, Seven Ave Marias, Gloria Patri

Fourth Sorrow: The Prophecy of Simeon
And Simeon blessed them and said to Mary his mother, "Behold, this child is set for the fall and rising of many in Israel, and for a sign that is spoken against (and a sword will pierce through your own soul also)." (Luke 2:34–35)

Fourth Joy: The Son Is Recognized as the Awaited Messiah
And coming up at that very hour she gave thanks to God, and spoke of him to all who were looking for the redemption of Jerusalem. (Luke 2:38)

Grace of the Mystery: the virtue of justice

Meditation on Simeon's prophecy: "A sword will pierce through your own soul also" (Luke 2:35):

Joseph traveled with his spouse to the temple to offer the Child to the Father, certainly not only to fulfill a legal prescription, but above all to manifest the fulfillment of the prophecies: Jesus is the angel who enters the temple, the one who will purify and rebuild the temple in the days of His Passion and death. The presentation and consecration of Jesus in the temple is the dawn of the Redemption, its official manifestation to all peoples. Indeed, Simeon designates Jesus as "a light for revelation to the Gentiles, and for glory to thy people" (Luke 2:32). This same old man, who had faithfully awaited salvation, speaks to Mary, and through her to Joseph, who was absorbed in prayer and his silent offering: Christ is the sign of contradiction. Those who believe in Him are saved, but those who reject Him are condemned. Many will be those who will try to contradict Jesus, to reject Him, to expel Him from His "property." They will inflict a harsh martyrdom on Him. In the days of His flesh, the Son will offer prayers and supplications with loud cries and tears (see Heb. 5:7). Joseph already "sees" all this. He experiences it in these words of Simeon which, like a fiery dart, pierce his heart. The sword of compassion that will rend Mary's heart will also reverberate vehemently in his heart. Joseph's virginal heart is now pierced by the sorrow of knowing with absolute certainty what awaits his Jesus. "Joseph, a sword will pierce your soul too": this is the echo of Simeon's words which reverberates just after these words are spoken to Mary. How could it be otherwise? Joseph's heart, given over entirely to Jesus and to Mary, beats solely for them, with them. The sorrow of Jesus and Mary is the sorrow of Joseph. His sacrificial obedience is enacted by taking the child and His mother with him (Matt. 2:14), and its inmost essence is expressed by his adoring silence. However,

Joseph also rejoices. The Son has been recognized as the awaited Messiah. Prophecies are being fulfilled. The temple doors have opened to welcome the Redeemer. Those who are moved by the Holy Spirit, like Joseph himself, will not have the slightest shadow of a doubt about who Jesus truly is. Joseph offers Jesus to the world. He gives the Savior to all mankind.

Pater Noster, Seven Ave Marias, Gloria Patri

Fifth Sorrow: The Flight to Egypt

And he rose and took the child and his mother by night, and departed to Egypt. (Matt. 2:14)

Fifth Joy: Joseph Is Consoled by God's Providence and by Jesus' Presence

God will provide himself the lamb for a burnt offering, my son. (Gen. 22:8)

Grace of the Mystery: the virtue of courage

Meditation on the flight to Egypt:

In the dead of night, the angel came to Joseph in his slumber and told him to make haste, to take the Child and His Mother and flee to Egypt. Herod was searching for the Divine Infant, seeking to kill Him. That helpless

Infant, who was now learning how to pronounce His first words, was already making the powerful tremble with fear, those whose souls were darkened by their lust for power. Hardly had the Truth been born when hatred for Him was also born. The darkness always attempts to stifle the light, to overshadow that Child. Now Joseph's mission is a mission of salvation. He must save the Savior of humanity. The devil urged Herod to kill Jesus. If He had died before his time, surely it would have been a victory for the devil, of the one who has always attempted to ruin the divine plans.

Joseph had been chosen as the protector of Jesus, His faithful guardian. He protects Him. He frees Him from danger. He shields Him with his life, with his heart, with all his love. The marriage with the Blessed Virgin had been willed by Heaven precisely as a means to confound the devil by hiding the virginal birth, the identity of Jesus, true man and true God. Joseph obeys the angel. In the middle of the night, he rises and immediately sets off to save his two treasures. He prepares to face a journey into the unknown, to a foreign land, distant not only geographically but also culturally from his homeland. Egypt had been a place of punishment for Israel, from which it had been miraculously liberated. Might it reveal itself to still be hostile to a Jewish family? There was no telling. Might it be a hospitable place? This Joseph hoped for, but in the meantime, his heart groaned, suffered. Uncertainty and discouragement might have gained the upper hand, but he was a strong, virile man. He obeyed and left, without delay. He trusted in his God, knowing that everything was in His hands, and set off with Mary and Jesus on their journey.

Long days, long halts awaited them. Amid groans and who knows how many tears upon seeing himself helpless most of the time, he never ceased trusting in divine providence. He remembered, deep down, Abraham's words to his son Isaac: "God will provide himself the lamb for a burnt offering, my son" (Gen. 22:8). He said this to Jesus in his prayers and thus comforted himself as well as comforting his Jesus. His prayer turned his bitterness and grief into heavenly joy and bliss. God had provided the Lamb for His People, for Egypt, and for every man of good will. Finally, they succeeded in settling in that foreign land. They found a makeshift accommodation. Between hardship and poverty, he endured the harsh winter of that exile. Jesus was with him and he with Jesus.

Pater Noster, Seven Ave Marias, Gloria Patri

Sixth Sorrow: The Return from Egypt
  But when he heard that Archelaus reigned over Judea in place of his father Herod, he was afraid to go there, and being warned in a dream he withdrew to the district of Galilee. (Matt. 2:22)

Sixth Joy: Joseph Finds Respite in Nazareth, Where He Can Serenely Contemplate His Son
  And when they had performed everything according to the law of the Lord, they returned into Galilee, to their own city, Nazareth. (Luke 2:39)

Grace of the Mystery: the virtue of fidelity

Meditation on the return from Egypt, the threat of Archelaus, and the decision to settle in Nazareth:

Joseph remained in Egypt until Herod's death. The bloodthirsty king of Judea in the meantime had ordered the death of all the firstborn sons of Bethlehem and its surroundings, aged two years and under. The heartrending echoes of mothers and fathers afflicted by so much cruelty resonated as far as Egypt. Joseph heard them. His heart was torn with grief. All those innocent children were martyrs of Christ, and Joseph gathered all the suffering in his heart and offered it all to the Father. He offered his lengthy sojourn far from his homeland and the suffering caused by his being a wanderer in order to protect Jesus. Finally, the cruel tyrant died, and Joseph, instructed again by the angel, was able to return to his country with the Child and His Mother. A long, wearisome journey awaited him once again. He undertook this arduous task joyfully because he was bringing the Savior back to His homeland. He was giving back to his homeland its Bridegroom, to his people their Messiah. Just as he was nearing that blessed land, he learned that Archelaus, son of Herod the Great, had been established by his father ethnarch of Judea; he was afraid to remain there, fearing that the father's cruelty might still be alive in the son, who was accused, moreover, of mismanaging his kingdom and of resorting to ferocious methods of repression. So he decided to return to Nazareth, where he initially came from. Still so much fear due to the threats that hung over the life of Jesus! He had thought that the time of exile, of hiding, was over. And yet those who threatened the life of the Son were always lurking about. The devil would always be ready to take the life of that Little One if he knew with certainty that He was the Son of God. Joseph, through his exorcistic action, prevents him from doing so. He conceals the divine Sonship from Hell. He conceals Him from the devil by presenting himself as a natural father, so as to deceive the devil, while nonetheless acting as a supernatural father, as guardian of the Son and the Mother. Joseph is the keeper of God's treasures. For Jesus and Mary, he was ready to sacrifice his whole life, and in fact, he did so at every moment. He does so even now, by adding another long stretch to that endless journey in order to return to Nazareth where he can finally find some peace. Home at last in Nazareth, more secluded and remote from political intrigues and hectic life than Jerusalem or even Bethlehem, he found peace. He sighed when he finally caught sight of its walls once again. They now had a roof over their heads. A modest little house it was indeed, but homely and safe. He felt as if he had gone through centuries of struggle and resistance. Every hour of exile lived in fear of losing his dear Jesus had seemed endless. Now he could devote more time to the serene contemplation of his son. He adored Him. He prostrated himself at His feet and offered his whole heart to Him. All his anguish. Now he could finally have some rest, while nonetheless always remaining vigilant. His heart remained wide awake. And he found his repose in God.

Pater Noster, Seven Ave Marias, Gloria Patri

Seventh Sorrow: The Loss of the Child Jesus in the Temple
And when they did not find him, they returned to Jerusalem, seeking him. (Luke 2:45)

Seventh Joy: Joseph Understands His Role as Earthly Presence of the Father and Patron of the Church
After three days they found him in the temple, sitting among the teachers, listening to them and asking them questions; and all who heard him were amazed at his understanding and his answers. (Luke 2:46)

Grace of the Mystery: the virtue of patience

Meditation on the loss of the Child Jesus in the temple:

Joseph was aware that he was merely the shadow on earth of the Father in Heaven. And now he experiences this. The Virgin Mary highlights Joseph's true fatherhood when, with those loving words, she presents to Jesus all their sorrow as parents distressed by his disappearance: "Your father and I have been looking for you anxiously" (Luke 2:48). "Where have you been, Jesus, my son?" Joseph repeats in the silence of his heart. This is the heart and soul of silence: an inexpressible sorrow, not externalized but suffered in silence and only sketched out through those words of the Mother. This was the greatest sorrow of the Purest Heart of St. Joseph, according to Fr. Stefano M. Manelli, these three days of frantic searching. Losing Jesus had been like dying. Without Him, the life of Joseph and Mary was, as it were, devoid of meaning. He is the Logos, He is the Meaning. Joseph is truly a father, but on a higher plane than human generational fatherhood. "All the more father as all the more chaste," St. Augustine would say. It is a spiritual fatherhood that hones suffering even more and makes it more excruciating. This, then, is the meaning of Jesus' words in response to His Mother: "Did you not know that I must be in my Father's house?" (Luke 2:49). The heavenly Father has primacy over everything and everyone. He comes before the earthly Father, before the Mother. Joseph now even more clearly discovers his true role: to be the shadow of the eternal Father, hiding himself to make room for Him. Between the heavenly Father and Joseph, there is a strong likeness. both generate that Son in a spiritual way; Joseph can generate Him because the

Father has begotten Him from all eternity. Joseph must remain within the Father's generation and thus will be a true father. Thus, his sorrow is transformed into love, his anguish at the loss of Jesus into joy, as he discovers what, deep down, he had always longed to be: the presence of the Father, the shadow of Heaven, the earthly silence of the generation of the Son in the silence of eternity. Joseph, however, also knows that those three days of anxious searching represent the three quintessential days in the life of Jesus: the mystery of His Passion, death, and Resurrection. Three days by means of which the temple, destroyed in the sacrifice of His body, will be rebuilt by the Son on the wondrous morning of the Resurrection. The Passion of Jesus has now been fully revealed, and so, too, his paternal cooperation. Joseph understands ever more clearly that the loss of the twelve-year-old Jesus prefigures much more to come. He unites himself to the will of God. He had embraced the trial of obedience, which is now shown to him in a new light: he is called to participate with Jesus in the restoration of the temple of God, of the new Israel, of the Church. He is, in fact, the patron of the Church.

Pater Noster, Seven Ave Marias, Gloria Patri

On the final trio of beads:

Hail Joseph by St. Louis-Marie Grignion de Montfort
Hail, Joseph the just, Wisdom is with you; blessed are you among all men and blessed is Jesus, the fruit of Mary, your faithful spouse. Holy Joseph, worthy foster-father of Jesus Christ, pray for us sinners and obtain divine Wisdom for us from God, now and at the hour of our death. *Amen.*

Pater Noster

Purest Heart of Joseph, in union with the Immaculate Heart of Mary and the Sacred Heart of Jesus, pray for us!

Bibliography

In order not to burden the text too much, as well as to facilitate the development of a long meditation on the figure of the Saint of Nazareth, we have preferred not to indicate throughout all the works consulted and cited. We now endeavor to offer the reader a list of the latter, along with some other books we would recommend—chosen among many—which can serve to expand the knowledge of a saint who, as has been repeatedly highlighted, after Jesus and Mary, has no equal in terms of his holiness and of his mission.

Magisterium[30]

Benedict XV. Motu Proprio *Bonum sane.* July 25, 1920. AAS 12 (1920): 313–317.

Benedict XVI. Marian Prayer of the Angelus. December 18, 2005. *Teaching of Benedict XVI* 1 (2005): 1002–1005.

[30] For an exhaustive Josephine bibliography on the Magisterium of the Supreme Pontiffs, beginning with Blessed Pius IX, see the doctoral thesis of G. A. Mattanza, "San Giuseppe, capo della Santa Famiglia, nel magistero pontificio dal Pio IX ai nostri giorni: L'importanza di San Giuseppe per la figura del padre di famiglia" (Ph.D. diss., Eupress FTL-Cantagalli, Lugano-Siena, 2019), pp. 605–693.

Francis. Apostolic Letter on the Occasion of the 150th Anniversary of the Declaration of St. Joseph as Patron of the Universal Church *Patris corde*. December 8, 2020.

John XXIII. Homily for the Canonization of St. Gregory Barbarigo. May 26, 1960. In *Discourses, Messages, Conversations of the Holy Father John XXIII*, vol. 2 (October 28, 1959–October 28, 1960), 355–365.

John Paul II. Apostolic Exhortation on the Person and Mission of Saint Joseph *Redemptoris custos*. August 15, 1989. AAS 82 (1990): 5–34.

Leo XIII. Encyclical Letter on Devotion to St. Joseph *Quamquam pluries*. August 15, 1889. In *Acta Papae Leonis XIII*, vol. 9, 175–183.

Pius IX. Apostolic Letter *Inclytum patriarcham*. July 7, 1871. AAS 6 (1870–1871): 324–327.

——. Decree *Quemadmodum Deus*. December 8, 1870. AAS 6 (1870–1871): 193–194.

Pius XI. Last Address Delivered in the Consistorial Hall on the Heroic Virtues of the Venerable Joan Elizabeth Bichier Des Ages. March 19, 1928. In *Speeches of Pius XI, S. E. 1., vol. 1, 1922–1928*, 779–780.

Fathers of the Church

Ambrose. *Expositio Evangelii secundum Lucam, 2, 6. Patrologia Latina* 15, 1555.

——. *Expositio Evangelii secundum Lucam, 8, 74. Patrologia Latina* 15, 1788.

——. *In Psalmum 118 Expositio, 7, 24. Patrologia Latina* 15, 1289.

Aphraates. *Demonstration 21, 9.* In Philip Schaff and Henry Wace, eds., *Nicene and Post-Nicene Fathers*, Second Series, vol. 13, p. 396. Buffalo, NY: Christian Literature, 1890.

Augustine. *Contro Fausto*, 23, 8. *Patrologia Latina* 42, 470.

——. *De consensu Evangelistarum*, 2, 1, 3. *Patrologia Latina* 34, 1072.

——. *Epistola 153*, 4, 9. *Patrologia Latina* 33, 657.

——. *Sermo 51*, 6, 9. *Patrologia Latina* 38, 338.

——. *Sermo 51*, 13, 21. *Patrologia Latina* 38, 345.

——. *Sermo 51*, 20, 30. *Patrologia Latina* 38, 350–351.

——. *Sermo 82*, 7, 10. *Patrologia Latina* 38, 510–511.

Basil. *Homilia in sanctam Christi generationem*, 4. *Patrologia Latina* 31, 1463–1466.

Hilary of Poitiers. *Commentarius in Matthaeum*, 2, 1. *Patrologia Latina* 9, 924.

Jacob of Sarug. *Homily on the Nativity of the Lord*, vv. 768–770. In Constantino Vona, ed., *Omelie mariologiche di S. Giacomo di Sarug*, n.s., 19.1–4, 221. Rome: Facultas Theologica Pontificii Athenaei Lateranensis, 1953.

——. *Verses*, 207–360. In Constantino Vona, ed., *Omelie mariologiche di S. Giacomo di Sarug*, n.s., 19.1–4, 143–147. Rome: Facultas Theologica Pontificii Athenaei Lateranensis, 1953.

Jerome. *Commentaria in Evangelium Matthaei*. 1, 1, v. 19. *Patrologia Latina* 26, 24.

——. *Commentaria in Evangelium Matthaei*. 2, 12, 49–50. *Patrologia Latina* 26, 84–85.

——. *De perpetura virginitate B. Mariae: Adversus Elvidium*, 15–22: *Patrologia Latina* 23, 198–206.

John Chrysostom, *Homilia in Matthaeum* 4,6; 5.3; 8.3: *Patrologia Graeca* 57.46, 58, 85–86.

Justin. *Dialogue with Trypho*, 78. *Patrologia Graeca* 6, 657C.

Origen. *Homilia XVII: In vigilia nativitate Domini. Patrologia Latina* 95, 1164C (attributed to Origen).

——. *Homilia in Lucam VI. Patrologia Graeca* 13, 1814–1815.

——. *Homilia in Lucam XIII. Patrologia Graeca* 13, 1832c.

Paulinus of Nola. *Poemata 25*, vv. 161–173. *Patrologia Latina* 61, 636–637.

Peter Chrysologus. *Sermo 145: De generationi Christi et de Joseph Mariam dimittere volente*. *Patrologia Latina* 52, 588–591.

——. *Sermo 146: De Ioseph sponso, et sponsa matre*. *Patrologia Latina* 52, 592–593.

——. *Sermo 175 : De Marcellino episcopo et de Virginis partu*. *Patrologia Latina* 52, 657–658.

Authors

Calloway, D. H., *Consecration to St. Joseph: The Wonders of Our Spiritual Father*. Stockbridge, MA: Marian Press, 2020.

Baij, C. M. *Vita del glorioso patriarca san Giuseppe*. 1st ed. Edited by P. Bergamaschi, 1921; repr. Rome: Edizioni Fiducia, 2021.

Bernardine of Siena. *Sermon on St. Joseph*.

Bulbeck, R. The *Doubt of St. Joseph*. *Catholic Biblical Quarterly* 10, no. 3 (1948): 296–309.

De Fiores, S. *Giuseppe di Nazaret*. In *Dizionario di Mariologia*, p. 587. Cinisello Balsamo, Italy: San Paolo, 2009.

Filas, F. L. *Joseph Most Just: Theological Questions about St. Joseph*. Milwaukee, WI: Bruce, 1956.

Garrigou-Lagrange, R. *De praestantia Sancti Joseph inter omnes sanctos*. *Angelicum* 5, no. 2 (1928): 195–212.

——. *The Mother of the Saviour and Our Interior Life*. St. Louis, MO: Herder, 1949. Originally in French: *La Mère du Sauveur et de notre vie intérieure*. Paris : Ed. Du Cerf, 1948.

Isolani, Isidoro. *Summa de donis Sancti Ioseph*. Rome: 1522; consultation of a reprint of 1888.

Keller, J. A. *St. Joseph's Help, or Stories of the Power and Efficacy of St. Joseph's Intercession*. United States: AMDG, 2015; original, London: Washbourne, 1905.

Lépicier, Alexis-Henri-Marie. *Tractatus de Sancto Joseph, Sponso Beatissimæ Virginis Mariæ.* Paris: 1908; 3rd ed., Rome: 1933.

Manelli, S. M. *Il mese di San Giuseppe: Meditazioni per ogni giorno del mese di marzo.* Frigento, Italy: Casa Mariana Editrice, 2018.

Mattanza, G. A. "San Giuseppe, capo della Santa Famiglia, nel magistero pontificio dal Pio IX ai nostri giorni: L'importanza di San Giuseppe per la figura del padre di famiglia." Ph.d. diss., Eupress FTL-Cantagalli, Lugano-Siena, Italy, 2019.

——. *San Giuseppe, un santo da riscoprire: Percorsi biblici, storici, sistematici e pratici.* Pessano con Bornago, Italy: Mimep Docete, 2021.

Newman, J. H. *A Triduum to St. Joseph.* In *Prayers, Verses and Devotions, pp. 320–322.* San Francisco: Ignatius Press, 2019.

Patrignani, G. A., S.J. *Il devoto di San Giuseppe.* Venice: 1724.

Pitre, B. *Jesus and the Jewish Roots of Mary: Unveiling the Mother of the Messiah.* New York: Image Books, 2018.

Scognamiglio Clá Dias, J. *San Giuseppe: Chi lo conosce?.* Rome: Heralds of the Gospel, 2017.

Stramare, T. *La vita di san Giuseppe: Spiritualità giuseppina.* Roma: Edizioni OCD, 2001.

——. *Gesù lo chiamò padre: Rassegna storico-dottrinale su san Giuseppe.* Città del Vaticano: LEV, 1997.

——. *San Giuseppe: Dai Padri agli Scrittori ecclesiastici fino a san Bernardo.* Naples: EDI, 2021.

——. *San Giuseppe: Dignità, Privilegi, Devozioni.* Camerata Picena, Italy: Shalom, 2008.

——. *San Giuseppe: Fatto religioso e teologia.* Camerata Picena, Italy: Shalom, 2018 (with another bibliography by the same author in light of *Redemptoris Custos*).

——. *San Giuseppe: "Il Custode del Redentore": Testo e riflessioni.* Casale Monferrato, Italy: Piemme, 1990.

——. *San Giuseppe nel Mistero di Dio*, Casale Monferrato, Italy: Piemme, 1993.

——. *San Giuseppe nella storia della salvezza: La pienezza del tempo*. Leumann, Italy: Elle Di Ci, 1993.

Thompson, E. H. *The Life & Glories of St. Joseph*. Charlotte, NC: TAN Books, 2013; original, London: Burns & Oates, 1888.

About the Author

Fr. Serafino M. Lanzetta is a Marian Franciscan based in the UK. He holds a doctorate in sacred theology (2008) with a thesis on Our Lady's Priesthood, and a post-doctoral habilitation in ecclesiology (2014), with a thesis on the hermeneutics of the Second Vatican Council. He is a lecturer in systematic theology at St. Mary's University in Twickenham, London, and at the Theological Faculty of Lugano, Switzerland. He has published a number of books and theological essays, covering several areas of systematic theology. He is also a broadcaster.